The Night Horse

ALSO BY WILLIAM REICHARD

An Alchemy in the Bones

The Brightness

How to

Sin Eater

As Breath in Winter

Two Men Rowing Madly Toward Infinity

The Night Horse

New and Selected Poems

by

William Reichard

BRIGHT
HORSE
BOOKS

Brighthorse Books
13202 North River Drive
Omaha, NE 68112

ISBN: 978-1-944467-10-4

Author Photo © Doug Baulos
Cover Design: Kailyn Hill
Cover Photo: Detail from "Cheval blanc monté, 1886," by
　　　Étienne-Jules Marey, [Public domain], via Wikimedia
　　　Commons

For permission to reproduce selections from this book and for
more information about Brighthorse Books and the Brighthorse
Book Awards, visit us on the web at brighthorsebooks.com.

Brighthorse books are distributed to the trade through Ingram
Book Group and its distribution partners. For more information, go
to https://ipage.ingramcontent.com/ipage/li001.jsp. For informa-
tion about the Brighthorse Prize, go to https://brighthorsebooks.
submittable.com/submit.

For James Cihlar and Viola Reichard

Contents

from *An Alchemy in the Bones* (1999)

An Alphabet

The branch, blanketed in ice, finishes in brittleness
and twigs scatter in the snow, form ideograms;

how many words are there for cold? for hunger?
The wind is steep, strips every street clean of traffic,

the possibility of travel. I learn two more words.
The ice recalls an impression of every foot,

retains the pattern of weight, the measure
of each of us. This is a science of retention;

what the elements keep, what the body records
of others. My arms are a slate upon

which your fingers have written; I touch them
when you are not here, read the letters

you have inscribed, hear your absent words
repeated as I pillow out into the snow.

The Monster's Dream

Remarkable, that the skin has such resiliency,
that the mechanics of tendon and bone
bend to this extent.
Where is the magic of breath?
On winter mornings, I've watched people
breathe, and their breath pours
from their mouths in a solid cloud;
these people wake the air, the heavens
issue out of them in white vapors.
Once, a man was dipping water from a pool.
I crept behind him and looked
over his golden shoulder;
it was the symmetry that startled me,
the color of his eyes, blue
as if the sky had nested inside.
When my face rested in his
on the silver surface of the water,
the way it only can in water, he screamed.
I had never stood so close to a man before.
What I remember now is the way his mouth
moved as he spoke, the scent of his breath
like sweet fruit and soil, the surface of the pond
as our twin faces shattered,
the way his blue eyes spread out and out
as the ripples sought the farther shore.

The Cloud Game

The clouds carry in another of June's remonstrances. Last week
the wind blew so hard a single strand of straw was driven
through a window without breaking the glass. We take

our meanings where we find them: eyes in the sky; the face of God
in the clouds; the visage of Christ in a hand towel or the bark
of a tree. On the hill, in Medjugorje, where the sun dances

and the Virgin speaks, not one rock or pebble remains.
Pilgrims have carried them off, hoping to be healed or at least
reminded of faith. When I was ten, the sky turned gray, then green,

and the wind screamed in the trees. When I emerged
from the basement, I found an apple tree sitting in a garden
where none grew. In those few minutes under the stairs,

I prayed, and God or something spared the house that is today
fallen into ruin. Perhaps I didn't pray hard enough, and only delayed,
but not denied, that final destruction. In the ceiling of the room

where I grew from child to man, I play the cloud game, searching
in the water stains that daily grow for some report from heaven,
a face in the plaster which comforts as it collapses, a guarantee

for anyone under that roof that she or he will sleep safe,
that the worst of what the heavens offer will be stayed,
the sternest of salvation's sky spared them.

Slow Meditation

The rock, white with guano where the pelicans nest,
looked like a pale ship caught in low tide.

The summer's shore gave up nothing but
some broken sand dollars and star fish, clinging

colorless and living in the tide pools at the base of the rocks
the locals called *The Three Sisters*. As in Chekhov,

they whispered secrets, and their waiting was painful.
That summer, someone had been shooting seals.

Oily black messengers of the sea, swimming
just close enough to the surfers to be mistaken

for those young men in slick black suits on their boards,
each black head bobbing in the cresting and receding waves.

No one knew who was killing them, or why.
Some said fishermen, angry and tired of sharing their catch.

Some said thrill-seeking teens, looking for that lasting surge
in a world devoid of the need for hunting.

Some said the surfers themselves, tired of those pointed faces
staring back at them like mirrors in the frigid water.

I was living in the Headlands then, in a valley cupped
by barren hills, an echo chamber for the sea and the animals

in recovery at the Marine Mammal Research Center,
one valley away. At night, I went to sleep to the cries

of seals and otter, eucalyptus creaking, my house
surrounded by a grove of those trees which

the Indigenous Plant Society members threatened
to eradicate in the name of floral purity. Walking on the beach

on the day of the Daisy Eradication—the Society's members
swarming the hills with black bags and trowels, uprooting

the unwanted immigrants from their foothold in the foothills—
I found a murdered seal. He was lying quietly, sleeping to

my untrained eyes, but frightening, sleek, sand crusting
his tender belly. Yet, not breathing. The stench was enormous,

and between his two closed eyes was a third, open orifice,
jagged, irregular, bloody but dried now, massing with flies,

the hole where his life had looked out at the sea, then fled,
leaving a swelling, dead carcass behind. The gulls circled

cautiously. On the bluff above, a vulture sat and waited for me
to leave and I wondered: Is all life based on such economy?

Living and dying, feasting and starving? I stood on that beach
with the need that had carried me to California, the hunger

for sun in a city blanketed by fog, the will to leave
the constant threat of winter's sleep. And still, I was unfed,

and even the birds knew more about finding what they needed
than me, a landlocked boy who had grown up away from the water,

who couldn't recognize death, who had never even learned to swim.

Without Translation

With sewn lips he speaks
        in a dazzling code that I cannot translate.

But the body has other mouths from which to speak,
        and these, I do comprehend:

How the blade of the shoulder has a tongue,
        and speaks.

How the abdomen, sweetly heaving, has a tongue,
        and speaks.

And the legs stretching, twining, have their language of muscle,
        and speak.

I wish I had a key, the proper code to unlock
        the door to his desire,

a dictionary to decipher the distance
        which my mind cannot span,

but my dry heart, my lips, my clumsy instinct,
        can.

Chromatism: Brown

In the country, in my mother's town,
flags are the new thing. Flying from the tops
of garages, the fronts of porches;
prefabricated family coats of arms
collected from cartoons with
your own special message to the world:
Hello! from Minnie. Hello! from Mickey.
Hello! from the cat with one paw raised
in recognition of the Buddha.
Hello! from the Buddha.
In November, everything is browned down
to one infinite shade. It's the cloudiest month.
I sit at the window in my mother's house
and look out at the street I grew up on.
A brown car passes. Someone has cut down
some trees I remember. Someone else
has placed a ring of stones around their yard,
encircling their house like a plain, brown temple.
In the kitchen, the turkey is browning
and my mother and sisters are blowing smoke
from their clouded lungs. My mother coughs
and it's a wet sound, brown, round, drowning.
From the peak of her garage her flag is flying.
Maybe our family coat of arms, though no one
has ever explained the symbolism to me:
A cat, a dog, a horse, a cow, all smiling,
marching en masse on a field of red and blue,
the word "Welcome" supporting them.
The color of the flag is startling, red against
a sky that, though blue, looks brown.

It's like a cardinal sighted in winter,
just outside your window: red against
that unforgiving field of white;
crimson, vivid, shining.

Rodeo Beach, California
Creation

At night, there is no delineation, only gradations
of gray and black, rhythm and sea.
Waves draw an aural measure between
blind land, blind water, bend rocks back to recede,
subtly, with each tide. There is nothing to look at.
My bare feet curl to meet the surface of each stone.
The fog breathes and I breathe with it, until
a solid flesh is reprieved; no lines stand between
skin and the invisible water, no definition, only
unmaking, the way the world dissolves sometimes,
when we cannot put our fingers on the true soul
of the mystery. For instance, creation.
What the water knows it will not tell.
What the pall teaches is only a dissolution of boundaries,
how night and fog can erase a world we comprehend,
rob our memory of well-traveled paths until
we cannot grasp origins, remember only
that it was always dark, then, in the beginning,
love came into the world, and with it, loneliness.

A Measure

"It's unlucky to know you're happy;
it's unlucky to say you're happy.
Touch wood. Cross my fingers. Spit."
        Jean Rhys, from Voyage in the Dark

It startles me: the intricacy of emotion,
the constant navigation, the willful amnesia.
Every morning and every night, my love,

I tell you I love you and leave you
something of myself. Every day
I go on to work and earn something back,

but these are never the same things;
there is never an equivalency, never a balance.
Once, when I was twenty-three, I believed

I had found the right man because
he lived in a loft and lead such
a bohemian life. Every night we made love

in a bed braced at the edge of a balcony,
a mirror propped against the opposite wall
and he would watch us as we grappled.

Somehow, he managed to live
both inside and outside his body
at the same time. I didn't understand then

why he left. Today, I know a little more,
have forgiven a little more.
When I wake with you

or when I wake away from you
I still say "I love you" to your pillow,
to the dawn, to some part of the new day

between us. Always, there is an accounting,
a debt joyfully paid. Always, I awake
and hungry, give you something back.

For Liam, When He Grows Up

She told me she named him William, Liam for short for the Gaelic in him,
and now I should know, at least in name, I would live.

She would see to my legacy and I let it pass, though I did not care
to see a child called after me after most of the brandings I have worn.

Some days I sing lullabies to those unborn, all of my sons and daughters,
and I wait for the things I do not want: those children, that family, a wife.

Some days I wonder if my mind will change and I let the thought through
as I search for that particular desire, the longing for a child, in a chest

that does not accommodate the need. And some days (most days) I just sit;
content to seek what my love will bear, what his love will create with mine,

and there is never a child here, not from our twin hands.
She carries Liam in her arms and that sweet flesh, the flaxen hair

and water-blue eyes speak for her. Now, she has found a new voice
and it will carry and comfort her through another seventy years.

By then, I will be dead. I give her my proxy to bear all of my children:
William and Billy and Willy and Bill, faggot and cocksucker,

homo and queer. I will her my legacy of names and hates
and she passes on the small memorials: in the searing laughter

of a growing child; in cards sent at Christmas to "Dear Uncle Bill,
Dear funny uncle, I hope you are well."

Sleep

I count stars on the ceiling
long after he extinguishes the light.

I count stars on his sweet back,
naming each constellation of freckles

which dot the arch of his straight spine,
the scalp of his shoulders.

And always after he drifts to sleep,
I count the minutes out

on my curled hands and wait,
contented, but do not find rest.

I cannot sleep in his company:

in the risings of his chest,
in the singing of his sleeping breath;

I pull at his arm and draw him from the dark.
Then, he traces letters with his fingertips

on the pale skin of my abdomen,
sends blades slivering

through my stomach as I laugh,
and watch my skin,

his words there etched
in furrows I cannot erase.

A Torn Curtain

The morning smells like cigarettes again;
the woman upstairs smokes
on the back porch and I wake
to a remembrance of your breath.
There isn't frost in California often,
nothing to obscure the long view
from a third story window out onto
a skyline fronted by Duboce Park
and all of its dogshit.
Here, a tidal cold maps itself indifferently
across the frozen windows; I look out
at a face obscured by frost, flowing past
like the figure of someone glimpsed
through a torn curtain.
It is your face; it is the same face
passing down a hardwood hall
on the way to the kitchen
for morning potatoes and tobacco.
My senses make a book of memory
and I keep such a diligent catalog;
if you die now you leave behind
some record: a photograph
tacked loosely to a nail-eaten wall,
an empty pack of cigarettes,
the scent of spent matches and curry.

Mnemonic

He was making a catalog of all the things
he could still see; the list was diminishing

with the new loss of every lighted cell.
Hanging directly across from his bed

was the photograph of a pretty young man
who looked more dangerously young

than he was. Every morning broke with it:
a soft focus down on the crown

of pale white hair; flawless, closed-eye face;
a torso hairless, small nippled;

the model rose in uncontained edges
from the black frame of the photograph.

On the last morning, on the day the sun
disappeared and he would no longer distinguish

between daylight and fire, the photograph
would be there, the boy on his wall

like a still, enshrined lover burned
into the memory of an unreceptive lens.

This is all he wanted: a list of what his eyes
would no longer decipher, a memory of what

fingers alone would now have to read
from a small, dark catalog of beauty.

Cost of Living

I know he's been in the bathroom again,
left the light burning all night long,
like the limb of some illuminated tree
extending a single branch out to him
in the darkness. And maybe it was nothing,
just the last dregs of dinner or too much water
at bedtime; there never used to be this paranoia
about the toilet. He is inconsolable in his
other bed, says fevers keep him flying away,
night sweats keep him mean.
Sometimes, he sleeps in the bathroom.
I switch off the bulb on my way to the kitchen,
where he sits, drooping over crumpled news.
Not even in the morning can I be angry, not even
when he wrecks my paper, spills coffee.
I pull rumpled sheets from his hands, lay out
the comfort of ritual news. The mailman
drops packets through the door; the bills
have come today: phone, gas, electric.
Everything must be tallied new, expensive now
as medication and electricity make over our lives.
And he smiles, tired, as I add up the costs, wave
desperate debts in his face and beg
Can't you put out the light?
Can't you just put out the light?

This Is A Test, This Is Only A Test

A flash of green at the base of the white wall. "Triton Moon" it's called, just enough black mixed in, no yellow. We are going to paint, but need to live with the color for a day or two, something small, a swatch, just to make sure it doesn't clash with the furniture because who needs more discord these days? Who doesn't get enough of it from the newspapers? The television? Last week I went to a clinic downtown, the anonymous one where you make up a name and number for yourself and come back to get your results at some preordained time. They drew a vial of blood from my arm and I called it 5-28-25: the date of my mother's birth, and the irony wasn't wasted on me, the knowledge that, if I flunked this test, the results would kill both of us. The sun just now across the wall. I follow the light as it moves from white to green, and crouch down on all fours to examine the effect. As I bend my arm, a slight pain in the tender flesh of the inside of the elbow, where the needle went in. Now it's nothing more than a small red spot, and by next week, when I get the results, the red will be gone. But not the green. The color in sunlight is ravishing, startling, as if something underground has been uncovered, and in the sunlight, allowed to spring into life. By next week it will have spread, with roller and drop cloth, brush and tape. Will have spread all across the walls of this room.

Constellations

Today I'm too tired to get out of bed. Instinctively I grope my groin, my neck, under my arms. I seek mounds of raised flesh mined, tender, dull, stinging. And always I remember: Today could be the first day of the end of my life. I count constellations: Big Dipper, Small Dipper, Orion's Belt. I flunked astronomy and hated science in high school, though now I take a more active interest in some aspects of the medical profession. I count stars: one dozen, two hundred, three thousand, until my reading eyes ache. And always I remember, numbers are relevant; but one or one hundred or more than one thousand (I know people who have passed that portion alone with partners they cannot name) the numbers are nothing. This morning, one is as good as one thousand; one thousand just means more experience below my belt, a better chance of having slept with a celebrity, or somebody else's husband. Today I'm too tired to get out of bed. I run numbers through my head, count on the fingers of one hand my own paltry list of partners. And who could it be? If any have left a lasting impression in my scorched blood. Whose kiss, whose cock may have blessed me with a lethargy of dreams from which I will not awake? Hands steal down instinctively to my groin, to gain some darker proof for my exhaustion, begin the delicate dissection of every inch of my lymph nodes. This territory, I have come to know too well these past ten years, this territory mined, so soft, so dangerous to the touch. But I touch. And today, nothing explodes. I count one, two, three lack of lumps, let my hands go to wander other territories. Today, the constellations do not bloom in my skin, do not pour poison from my singing blood in any pattern I can trace. Today, I am still alive; the stars are on my side.

It Takes Me

some sort of a
                rhythmia takes me whenever I try to write about you
words and rhythm are never enough some sort of a
                        rhythmia takes me I fail to build the
better stanza fail to catch the music of the action of the phrase it
takes me: sitting in the car on a field road necking like there isn't skin
enough or time in the dormitory stretching out a hand to brush your
thigh by accident and stuck up against the wall you lift me take me
down in the ditch with an axle broken walk five white miles in January
it takes me: watching you drive from the back seat seeing some girl
get all over you like a lip-sticked snake it takes me: bent on the coffee
table fucked from behind like a cow mounted I whine and the wood's
crisp edge pressed a deep crease in the skin of my stomach some sort
of a
                                rhythmia
takes me trick memory tripping
        out
                of sequence it takes me ten years practice a
                            rhythmia
trampled I learn to balance I quietly back down and you join the faces
who fare no better than a photograph left in the sun my elephant's
memory stretches out to meet you I catalog everything everyone and
then you die and how can I draw a poem out of dissonance how can I
cut a poem from something that has no clean
                        breaks?
it takes me you die no poetry there no metrics and some sort of a
                            rhythmia
takes me some sort of halting cry of mourning done once and left to
die you can't be buried twice but you, you treat me to repetition live
again screaming in the trees and some sort of a

rhythmia takes me some treach-
erous kiss some cock some carnal coward who left me at nineteen
stripped and crying you trip me John for a decade you trick me every
time I pull my pants down let's admit it I never knew you knew only
the bones you wanted revealed never dug beneath the flesh never hap-
pened to find any discrepancies in the seams of your skin in the fit of
your clothes or your cock I cannot deny that stifling eye or the skill of
your pleasured body but what fit in the bedroom never worked on the
bus on the street with public life lived away from cum stained sheets or
words of love what made sense in the bedroom never makes sense now
in the funeral pyre some sort of a

rhythmia takes me every time I try
to translate you to paper to poetry I've lost your language you will not
make metrics for me now not even in your grave.

Now That We Are Never Finished Mourning

Don't even start. It would be a long, ugly list.
How one morning Mark couldn't wake up and we recall
his wondering aloud whether he might turn into ashes
in Wisconsin. How his remains were flown home
in a plastic jar, back to San Francisco, not the Midwest,
because Wisconsin (or Minnesota, or the Dakotas,
or Michigan, or Iowa…) is a place which, once left,
can never be convincingly returned to again.
How Brett took the ashes to the Detour
and dumped some on the floor, bits of bones
and fine gray powder ground under the heels
of well-worn leather boots. It was all accomplished
in darkness. Other ashes scattered in the park,
under the stands of rhododendron, used condoms,
cigarettes, old gum, and Mark, seeping down into
the city's unstable soil. Don't even start.
I don't know enough stories, or maybe only
beginnings, or ends; say, the details: the translucence
of a man's skin in the afternoon light, a bit
about his hair or his eyes. Their names can be
alphabetized, but never ordered; I can never
do justice to them, their capacity for knowing
each exact moment, each heated contact,
the taste, the scent, the texture of skin.
Don't even start. I could say it all again,
retell every story I've ever told and still
no one would listen. Why should they?
Aren't we all tired of death? It used to be
we'd tell a story and something, some lesson
or knowledge, would be made or unmade.

And something else would change. Now, nothing.
Now that we are never finished mourning,
the shapes, the intentions of the stories have changed
and we all walk away, uninterested or weary
or used up when we read the obituaries
or hear one more poet on the stage proclaim
   This poem is dedicated to the memory of...

A Widow's Song

Your body says this. The thin hair on your head says this.
The varicose veins in your legs say this. Your skinny limbs,

the brown spots on your arms.
In Nepal, a little girl is given the nut from a bellfruit tree

and married to a Hindu god so she will never be a widow,
never sleep in the thin embrace of remembrance.

If you should die, where is the place that I will call home?
It has taken me too long to believe in refuge,

to trust the sincerity of need and ardor.
If I sleep in your arms, let your arms be a promise;

my breath weaves a rope that pulls around us, binds us.
There was never a ceremony when I was a boy,

no promises made to a spirit that I would never be alone;
when I am old, be old with me.

There Be Monsters Here

Driving Sunday and suddenly the countryside I grew up in
is unfamiliar, the path from my mother's house to my sister's
unclear. Pulling to the side of a rough gravel road,

I open the glove, get out a map. For every one of eighteen years
I spent in this rural county, for every year I've spent since
running away, returning home, I should know these roads,

all paths that lead out from the forest, into the meat-steamed kitchen
where my mother resides, my fertile sisters at her feet.
But ten years in a city of neat, square blocks and buses,

rows of identical houses I can tell apart through
subtle differences, this has destroyed my sense of north, south.
I can no longer name any tree; and this map, senseless, might come

from the bottom of a sea chest or the floor of a tomb.
I turn it around and around like the wing of a windmill,
hope it will name a direction. I'm reminded of a class I took

as a freshman: Geography 101 and all of that history, those maps
the teacher held up from the Dark Ages and beyond, were fragile circles
stretched to encompass the whole world. But ancient cartographers

didn't have a large enough scope to complete their planet.
Trapped, they knew their own countries and the veiled regions
that bordered; and where there were places suspected to exist,

but uncharted, they drew fantastic creatures, cheeks puffed,
lips curled, blowing out the four winds and wrote
There be monsters here. In the yard of a farm across the road

I see three frayed children scrambling with an old tire, recall the smell
of hot summer rubber, the peeling texture of thin tread.
Those ragged strangers, aliens to me, scream at a dog, speak of everything

I have run so fast to forget. But with one last glance down the road
I am walking toward them, reminded of the fear of knowing,
of being left alone. The horizon sweeps up from gravel, vanishes

in the cloud of a passing pickup. So much dust to navigate
in the quiet country, so few farms like continents adrift in a sea
of wheat and corn. I call out ahead *Hello!* and wait for a reply.

The Window, Autumn

Outside, she rakes maple leaves into loose piles, stakes burlap and wire
around roses rarely coaxed to bloom. From inside, I watch my mother
through old windows as she is changed by the bend of the pane.

Old glass, slow as continents, drifts down over years,
pools at the bottom of the sill, and spreads the world out in a new
spectrum. Old glass, viscous as memory, runs unseen.

She moves on. The leaves sit in ordered mounds until the wind comes;
she begins to prune the hedges, collects grass at the base of the fence.
The summer starts to push away in the promise of a brittle breeze and

she cleans. She cleans. Outside, my mother is transformed,
a woman woven into the trees: her hands and face warped
and spread into the branches, a body bent and blending

across the lawn. Now, she knows a world without children,
lives in a place I've never seen. She stoops over, throws a stone
into the deep ditch, snaps down the brown milkweed.

Jerry Lee Lewis Kills His Child Bride

On the back roads of Blue Earth County, I rode in the open back of a
pick-up with my sisters, with three drunk brothers-in-law in the cab
taking turns pretending to steer. We called this joy riding, though my
throat was filling up with dirt, though my sister Linda sat propped
against the cab, wheezing through incomplete lungs, and the brothers-
in-law kept opening up the little window between inside and out and
offering us beers. Jerry Lee Lewis screamed out from the eight-track,
caught in the loop of track two, over and over again singing *Goodness
gracious great balls of fire!* My sisters discussed what they had just heard
on the news: that this star who played piano with his foot had been
accused of killing his wife, the one he married when she was thirteen.
My sisters dreamed of this

                    and I dreamed too

                              white trash grand
passion on the top of a big black piano, of a man like Jerry Lee coming
to lure us away from the next kegger; the death, we let slip by; it was
only an accusation. But I wondered about pianos, and saw Mrs. Jerry
Lee spread out in a pink chiffon dress, her petticoats covering the
whole surface of a piano-shaped swimming pool; on this dry day it had
to be a pool where she died, drowned with a martini in her hand. The
pick-up plunged down a hill. We all screamed, and Linda wheezed,
looking like a skinny fish; death before celebrity would be a shame.
And it's really only a matter of degrees that separates the famous white
trash from the unfamous; any one of my sisters could achieve a bee-
hive, pink chiffon formal, crinoline bigger than her whole body. Our
dreaming father bought a piano one day, on credit, and promised us
lessons.

    In the summer.

             But summer never came that year, and

I snuck lessons from a friend who said he wanted to be Vladimir Horowitz. I said I hadn't heard his songs, and could he play the piano with his foot? I managed *Fur Elise* before the creditors closed in for non-payment, and only managed to snatch my romance novels from the bench before they hauled the piano out the door. Our father said nothing. My sisters didn't notice. And I didn't care; the only time I really wanted to learn to play piano was when I watched the creditors carry the spinet down the steps, and load it into the back of their van.

Northern Light

Midnight and my mother walks
into the room where I sleep
with the television's blue glow.

She's just come off the evening shift
at the printing factory and small clots
of shaved paper cling to her clothes,

her ink-stained fingers.
She nudges me awake, her face
illuminated by the glowing end

of a cigarette. *Come outside* she says,
her eyes too animated for the late hour;
I obey, though I drag a blanket-

remnant of my sleep-behind me.
Late autumn cuts into my feet
as I walk onto the cement steps

and my mother points into the air
where the sky is alive with fire.
Color braids up in a wild cone

undulating, and light spills red,
green, blue, white
into the unaccustomed night.

Northern lights my mother says
and I am amazed as the factory drains
a little from her face, and I realize,

at this hour, in this strange light,
that it is almost possible
to believe in anything.

Fort Collins, Colorado

She has three appointments this morning alone with the dean's wife, the doctor, the man at the museum. Then the luncheon, the banquet, the faculty wives. Member of every social committee, she streams down the streets of her suburbia, station wagon well in hand, makes lists on a notepad pinned to the dashboard, stamps letters with a dry tongue and catches fuchsia, lavender, white blossom petals lining the streets in orderly rows; she steals a glance, makes a note to notice them before the end of the season. A truck rounds the corner; she's driving behind, and it's too sharp, too fast; truck wheels leave the ground; she locks brakes, drops pencil, stops making the list; she turns sideways, the truck sways nearly over and then back again to four wheels. She sits horizontal, spanning the road. The truck pushes on, unconcerned, only brushed the trees on the corner lawn and she feels them, the branches shaking, something vibrating up through earth and asphalt.
   This is no time for moving.
She clutches her pencil, points to the list and watches it snow; May, and it is snowing. *Fuchsia, lavender, white* she writes fast enough to capture the color of every flake. She writes *fuchsia, lavender, white* and the windows are down, the snow comes in and it is so warm for the season, so late for snow. She writes *fuchsia, lavender, white* until the pencil fades from her hand, the dashboard drops away and there is only pure color left before her eyes, drifting down through the sunroof, blowing in from the driver's side. She knows she should be cold. She knows about weather, but she has never seen this snow before, shaking from branches, her own storm. She sits, drops pencil, tips head back and lets it all come down fuchsia, lavender, white. Her arms are covered in petals, her lap full, her head crowned in *fuchsia, lavender, white*.
   This is no time for moving.

My Father Speaks

After he had been dead eight years, I couldn't remember
the sound of his voice, the tenor, the pitch, the Iowa inflection.
Maybe I never knew what he sounded like,

all of the years he was living, but moving away from me,
becoming memory before his body died. There is always
one price for forgetting, another for remembering;

the sound of his voice rides on the back of a memory
of his face, his hands large, fingers clicking together like sticks;
the dead, unrestful, unbury themselves

when we think too long on them, our thoughts
like a thin rope down into the earth, their pale hands
pulling up and up into an unaccustomed light.

A voice just now, through the window well;
a voice from the back yard, a voice from the trees.
It reminds me of someone. I cannot see who is speaking.

In the Lobby of the Hotel Saint Francis, San Francisco

Her gown, yellow-gold, fades in the afternoon light.
A debutante come to rest in the brocaded safety
of the hotel lobby, waiting, perhaps, for her party
to begin, waiting to be brought out, and thus, in,
to the arms of an eager, generous world.
Those who know enough to know are already
seeking her, their cameras offered like chests
filled with treasure for this newest, freshest goddess.
In the morning, the papers will be full of it:
Everyone who sat at her table. Everyone who
danced her dance. What they all wore.
The smartest of what the smartest said.
It will all be read with laconic grace by those
who could attend. With grave sincerity
by those who wanted to, but could not.
I can't recall her name at the moment.
I know I've seen her before, though
this new incarnation, newly emerging
in yellow and gold, has an adult's inclination
toward iciness. She sits in front of a window,
and outside, the raging garden coils in
upon itself, and the window frames the paths
and makes of them a study in contrasts:
A verdant painting, a canvas breathing
with the sunlight on her dress, the raucous red
of an amaryllis springing from a pot
behind her head. If I could say anything
I wanted at this moment, I'd probably sing.
The song would be quiet. No one would hear
the words. Just something brief, about blossoms,
their self-assured rapture, the secret
that is their serenity, in spring.

from *How To* (2004)

Babel

Everything wanted its own language.
Before the schism, everything
had one tongue, and that tongue
was one muscle in the one mouth
of the world, speaking one word
over and over.
          We can't remember it now.
Something to do with water, sky, stones, fire.
The intricacies implied, one raised eyebrow
or a nod between strangers on the street;
in passing glances, a whole story told.

Now we're all so specialized
the doctor for your left foot
can't look at your right,
and volumes are written on
every letter of a too extraneous
alphabet. Before, the story was
as simple as
         A
         only beginnings;
something to do with joy.

Hypothesis: Faith

If I say I can smell the storm coming on, he won't believe me.
Even if I cannot see it, even if my eyes are bound by
a heavy black cloth, the way a medium's eyes
were covered tightly in authenticating tests at the turn
of the last century. Now we're ready to turn again, a century older,
another millennium. This time, fewer seers, more saviors.
Never mind. The way to this world or the next is never clear.

If I say I can smell the rain as it hurries toward me,
though I haven't checked the charted warnings or radio forecasts,
he won't believe me. The ways of skeptics are proven,
worn smooth by years of patient disbelief. In 1899,
a woman in London could make tables rise, speak in tongues
in languages she'd never learned. A certain skeptic,
a wealthy gentleman, did his best to debunk her, tied
elaborate sets of strings to her arms and legs, a web
from which she could not escape without direct assistance
from the spirit world. Cameras ready, reporters from all
the world's major papers present, the spirit guides freed her.
The skeptic was a man transformed and asked her
there in the presence of the world to marry him.
                                    She declined.

If I tell him as we're walking that I know the rain is coming,
he won't believe me. Not with blue skies, summer sun,
his propensity to defeat any instance of doubt or faith.
He refuses to take his umbrella. Some things must stand on faith.
As we walk, we're drenched by a sudden, pounding rain and
he looks at me as if to say

mere coincidence

or

I'll learn to pray if you can offer further evidence.
But there is no need. My pants stick to my legs, my shoes
squelching and soggy. He needs to believe, but cannot.
I try to hide from faith. As we walk, I see a man emerging
from the rain, his umbrella raised. He smiles as he passes us,
and I smile back, pleased at this moment of contact
with someone who also knows the delicate, subtle life of the rain.

On a Scene From Kabuki

The stars on his robe run together like rivers.
The pattern of her silk forms paths

upon which he is lost. She's a shadow

under the cloth, in the half-light.
She keeps herself elusive, quick, sudden.

His hand, white, grasps the air

as if he could somehow hold it,
keep it, own it. She's hiding.

He holds the cover under which

she crouches, but pretends not to see her.
Under the cloth: darkness.

Under her robe's sash: a weapon,

concealed for *maybe* or *if necessary.*
The stars on his robe run together like shadows.

She's a river, quick, sudden.

Hypothesis: Love

In Dydima, in Turkey, she wades in a pool in the ruins of a temple
to Apollo. There the god's sibyl sat on a watery throne,
uttering prophecies from her master, offering guidance to those
who came seeking direction, and left with dictates both vague and
urgent:

> *Change the path upon which you now tread!*
> *Watch the way the wound will mend for a sign from the god,*
> *a shape, a letter, spelled out in the scar.*

As she moves through the shallow pool, she curls her toes sharply,
picks up a small stone. This is forbidden-the site's historic-
but she draws it up from the pool's floor, then slides her hand,
discreetly, into the elastic confines of her bikini bottom,
to remove later, at a safer distance from arrest.
Small plunder-one pebble-and she wants to send home
some link to the past, a talisman for a friend who seeks
too many answers in undependable stars. She watches
her husband in the pool. Pilgrims have come here for centuries,
seeking absolution or guidance. She wonders which he now seeks,
standing still in the water, the livid green reflection of sunlight on
moss making his face sallow, strained. They've come all this way,
thousands of miles from Minneapolis to Turkey, just to discover
they're breaking apart. She didn't need an oracle for that,
but he stands now as if listening to something, a voice, perhaps,
from a past filled with revelations:

> *Speak, Apollo. Show me the way to the exit. Drop me at the airport.*

Two months later, a package arrives in Minneapolis. Inside, a small
box, inlaid with shell; a batik scarf of gauze-like silk; a stone.
A note explains the origins of the rock and what I don't understand,
I ask her. She's been sleeping on my couch for weeks and has
no intention of going back. She can't bring herself to tell him.

I suspect he already knows, must sense in her sudden departure
a distance greater than the miles from Istanbul to home.
She's come carrying two cats with Turkish names, clothes,
some books, some rugs. Her finger's without a wedding band
and I don't ask. *Love*, she says, *can't live in isolation*.
The stone's smooth surface resonates with someone's history,
all of the stories of pilgrims who sought purpose in a pool in a cave.
Tell me more, I say, and she settles back with a beer and a cigarette.
It all began… she begins and I close my eyes and listen, her words
small but clear, echoing through my apartment like the voice
of a sibyl a thousand years away:

> *Speak, Apollo. Tell me what I came to hear.*
> *Tell me the joys and vagaries of love.*

Black Mountain, Ten Perspectives

One
These are the secrets I tell myself.

Two
The mountains are old. The woman I visit, Kitty,
old as the rocks from which she builds her home.
Ancient follows ancient; ancient settles into the hillsides
and the ancestors of our beliefs—not blood-tied mothers
and fathers, but those to whom we tie ourselves
with loyalty and purpose—settle into us; age progresses,
a thing owned or given; not grown, but earned.

Three
I am afraid of growing old.

Four
I'm afraid of *not* growing old.
Afraid my generation is dying, one hand
passing on in the promise of pleasured bodies
death to the other. Afraid of the euphoric amnesia,
the way we move the dying not toward,
but away from ourselves:
the fearful contagion of mortality.

Five
Every child knows these stories, memorizes them
as he washes, then buries, his father. Yet we do not
bury our fathers now, but our brothers, the men in whose arms
we learned the meaning of conquest and surrender.
Too much of these men resides within us,

too much for us to divest or disavow
before we give them up to the ground. For instance:
I've buried a lover, a man who played piano, let himself move
with rhythm and vengeance across two continents.
Now I'm watching two more die; men with educating arms,
eyes like fire, bodies never quiet in their insistent singing.

     Six
The wood bees burrow into the studs of the house,
hang outside the door and menace us.
Kitty, my ancient friend, says she has never been bitten,
is not afraid of the nature of bees.

     Seven
I'm afraid of nature.

     Eight
I'm afraid of my own body.

     Nine
My body
          in confusion
grew a pea-sized lump one day,
just above the most prominent rib on my right.
Mottled gray, blue veined, and dull to the touch.
          no pain
The doctor, as he cut away, was smiling,
while I felt something running down my side,
numb and wet. I smelled the burning flesh.
When he finished his job he held the tumor up

in the red steel teeth of his tweezers and said
Take a look!
Here it is!
Your benign baby!
But I could only look away, and count, patiently,
the even-spaced holes in the white tiled ceiling.

Ten
On the screens of windows of illuminated rooms, bugs massing.
As if the light within contains the last of earth and everywhere else
is water, and death.
Dreaming. Breathing. Heavy breathing.
Making babies. The way *they* do. In the next room.
In the room beyond that, my father sleeps and my sibilant mother
rocks in a trance of exhaustion; nothing comes from her lips this night
of any importance. Forget and the morning comes in a red dawn
with the requisite warning to sailors and all who toil on the sea.
But then, I started on the mountainside. At midnight.
Never near the water.
The trees were whispering. It was black out. I could hear their voices.
What was it they said?
In the dark.
Three cars passing, in quick succession.
In the dark.

Letter to a Friend in San Francisco

November here opens a door. You would recognize this,
having grown up, like me, in this colder climate.

Yesterday it was so warm I walked around the lake
in shorts and shirtsleeves. Birds flew in vast waves

over the water. Today, the wind rips at my jacket,
and my poor hands, barometers, begin to ache and freeze.

The days grow shorter. Nights, in gust and gale, prevail.
We all live inside. What I know of you in your new home

comes only second-hand, descriptions of a house
in the hills, a garden filled with fantastic, primordial plants,

a series of birds you've taught to speak so that
each day, when you return from work,

these pets call out to you like a lover or a parent
        Hello! Hello! Hello!

Forgive me if I embroider or invent the pictures:
You, on your hillside, looking out at the bay.

You, at the dockside, coiling rope onto the deck
of your small boat, seagulls crying overhead.

You, watching your lover drive away to a new home,
then collapsing, the way lovers do when a new door

opens onto memory, onto loss. I know he has been
with you for a decade. I've met him in other cities.

I have approved. Now, you sit in your exotic garden
alone, making phone calls home to this colder land

because that's all there is left to do, reach backward
for help, move forward as you can.

We mend where we may, and for you, there's nothing
I can say that would make sense. Only: this is what

loss is: emptiness; a way of not seeing
through the void. After we spoke,

in my own winter-bare garden, unseasonably warm,
my arms drank in the best of the sun.

I thought about us, our common past. More and more,
there is nothing I can do to help anyone, except listen.

All around me, in the trees, the birds that remained
were singing. Perhaps they were fooled

into believing we had all missed something wicked,
the long sleep of winter. Perhaps not.

They are so pragmatic, little birds;
the way they can recognize the order of things;

the way they can, even in winter, sing.

Thunder

Five-thirty, July, and it's dark.
All of the paperback covers are curling.
My hair curls, which always hangs
limp like a worn rope.
My door curls, the lock
threatening to snap
when I turn the bolt,
pull the warped door open.
My arms curl. Summer has come
and there you are in Chicago,
eight-hundred humid miles away.
My arms are empty;
their bones and muscles
have lost your shape.
It's getting darker.
No light to prepare dinner
and the flies mass
on the screen, dying
to be let in, to bite once.
Trees are going limp,
vacuum of the storm
sucking out the last hot winds.
Everything in the air stalls,
on my skin a thin membrane
of sweat and pollen.
Now the man next door
crosses the street to his car,
his steps shudder through still ground.
          Thunder's coming!
he promises an unseen companion.

He wears no shirt.
His hard chest shines
smooth with sweat.
The whole dark sky begins to shake.

Three Stories

One: A Lust Story

He has wanted the young man for three years and has finally told him.
He has been rebuffed.
This is never why.
The persistence of desire,
like hunger, like dreams; the need to take in something of the young
man, like a piece of hard, bitter bread.
This is never why.
The way that desire
spins small and sightless on the tips of his nicotine-yellowed fingers.
Too many cigarettes and clouds of smoke rise yellow
above his head.
This is never why.
Speaking of longing destroys something
of its architecture, the frame fragile, never sure, even when his desire
is built on the backs of other men who have never known
how to say no. Now, when he sees the young man, there is a hesitation
with him.
This is never why.
He's always been hesitant. But now
the young man knows and this forms a kind of circle.
The way he will do anything to set their lives back in balance;
the way he will never remember when to stop thirsting;
the way he's always dreaming, and hungry.

Two: A Love Story

How you danced into your dream! First you were dating a woman
named Jennifer and I was drinking too much

spent a night passed out on a bathroom floor because I'd had too many
    vodka tonics

and then you were bisexual and in love with a speed skater with a cute ass
and I still see him on local TV interviewing Lutheran bishops

I can't say I remember the way the cold tile felt on my face; how the grout
pressed a checkered design into the skin of my right cheek
and my secret boyfriend didn't bother to help me up but complained
when I couldn't cook breakfast in the morning

You stopped dating Jennifer and found the impossible true love in Chicago
and that was with a man long before the rest of us knew enough of
ourselves to allow love in

and the secret boyfriend went to Hungary and got AIDS and died
in our hometown a hero with a halo of whispered truths and prayer circles
his mother organized to ask for the miracle that would save her son's life

Our miracles were modest

Your husband of ten years likes animals and I think of the rat
he had when you met him, the one that died on the operating table

and I only ever got as close to a rat as the barrel of a bee-bee gun
      would allow
until college and then it was in a lab, tiled and clean, wearing rubber gloves
while I sliced in and noticed the way the bloodless skin looked
against the white glare of the tile

Maybe my dead lover was a rat too like you said a rat that fed and fed
my desire before he ended up in some other brighter tiled room

You never told me the rat's name only that your lover was broken-hearted
and the rat never woke from the anesthetic

Three: A Ghost Story

Suppose the notched wheel turns once, turns twice, and Dante's ratchet
       as my friend Natalie has it in her own heavenly vision
pulls him up and up, closer to the world you've made, the one
without him in it.
                        What would that be like?
                                              A ghost world filled
with sexless cartoon characters suddenly sprouting huge cocks
and crashing through your effete wonderland, fucking you from dusk
till dawn and still, you wouldn't have enough. Isn't that another way
of saying
              this is what happens when dreams come true?
                                              Every man is dead
and resurrected in his own time. He takes on his spectral body of sex
and dreams when his flesh is wasted. He always could go again and again
and again, exhausting you all night long. This is why you cannot sleep,
and if you sleep, cannot wake.

If he offers you something like unending love, don't take it. Better to
       shiver
through winter alone than to feel a hand closing over your own
on a night when you sleep by yourself. At dusk, walk to the river
and throw an iris in.
                        This will be for him, but nothing else.
                                              Let the water
carry your gift, like an offering, to wherever it is that he has found
to call heaven. Don't bother to speculate. When he comes to your room
                                              in dreams

and offers himself as a groom, decline. No one can afford
such heavy slumbering satisfaction. No one can fulfill such awful,
hungry desire. Kiss him once, just for memory. Allow yourself to admit
that you are always almost happy.

On the Prairie with My Father

The summer the rains never came
we went to the Badlands, where four
finished Presidents stared hard
and rocky across the hills at
an unfinished Indian, his giant arm
raised, pointing out toward still
disputed lands. I was a boy then,
and my father drove truck
cross country, delivering prefab houses
to happy people on the plains.
One man fed us steaks as we sat
on the poured concrete foundation
of his unfinished home, another
paid my brother and me a few cents
an hour to help unload itchy
pink insulation from the trailer
as our father disapproved and frowned.
All summer, what I wanted
was to be home, in the kitchen
with my mother, canning beans
and beets, eating bitter lettuce
and egg salads thick with mustard
and mayonnaise.
                          I still recognize summer
from its taste.
                          What I wanted
was the refuge of rhubarb leaves
and cool hedges, laundry on the line
and strawberries saved from ants
and crows. What I wanted

was to run from thunder
as it spread across the fields,
to cower in the weeds, to meet
the sun, blonde and blind and tanned
pale honey and chocolate, shocking
hair struck white from sunlight.
Instead I had the sleeper in the truck,
the heat of a semi on blacktop
and miles of road unwinding
across empty prairies until it seemed
the truck was standing still
and the scenery was spooling by
like a bad backdrop in an old movie.
One day, delirious from heat,
I swore I saw a horse and buggy
with a skeleton at the reigns,
but my father and brother wouldn't
believe me when I said death
was on the road. That night,
my father explained prostitutes
to us when a woman knocked
on the truck window and asked
if we needed company.
I don't think he used the word
prostitute. He didn't even
mention sex. But we knew,
my brother and I, initiated at
an early age into pleasure's secrets
by neighbor boys who whispered
some things and demonstrated others.

They come to keep you company
if you're lonely. That's what
my father said about the woman,
but that was enough. My father
didn't let the woman in

                      not that night
but I sensed he knew firsthand
what such women wanted,
what they had that he wanted
in return

          by then, my parents
hated one another, and who knew
where they each turned for sex—
I had been the last accident
of their mutual lust
and I was ten—

                  I knew even then
that a decade was too long
to wait for something you were
used to having, something
your whole body hungered for.

The Unexpected Universe

I'm beginning to believe
the first idea I had about the stars;
that the earth was a sphere

within a sphere and outside,
that was all light spilling out on us
when the sun slept,

piercing the outer shell
in a thousand gasping points.
Now I know pure reason spins

the earth on its axes,
burns the light of the stars
so bright that we only see

their labor backward through time,
know only the faces of light
which died millions of years

before we were born. And these stars,
these luminous ghosts,
are the science that dispels

my little myth of world within world,
the story of unreasonable reason displacing
the order of a less reasoned joy.

Hare

he took them out behind the apple trees and the sounds the silent things make
clouds casting rough shadows across concrete steps
the tide of traffic on the highway, a place in the fence just big enough
so I could crawl through into the deep ditch, the darkness of forgetfulness,
       grass blades, milkweed stalks, smooth like skin, like fingers

his knife, his two-by-four because that was more humane to knock them out
the scent of alfalfa and the taste of the clover I gathered for them
the purple round-headed flowers and the sweet flavor
the way the apple trees would soak up all the blood, the red red apples in the fall
       and all full of worms

I never ate them, and nothing tastes just like chicken that resembles a cat
that's lost its skin, their fur, just behind the ears, the softness of their necks
the way they would not shudder when I touched them when I fed them clover
the peace of a summer garden, my father's fingers, those heavy hands, a sense
       of darkness, weightlessness, the touch of the familiar

On the Pontoon

Summer on a borrowed pontoon,
drifting on a northern lake
with my brother, my sisters;
scent of cigarettes and beer,
stubs snuffed out
in almost-empty cans.
I feel the pattern of the iron floor
press into my back
like a template;
feel my panic rising
at the thought
that I am thirty-four
and have no job;
that the sky above us
shines just as blue
on some petit bourgeois
suburban heaven
but none of us here
could ever afford
those house payments.
The dirty old dog
my brother named Sam
barks and leaps into the lake,
the clear lake, and all around
the pontoon the water clouds.
Andy coaxes the dog on board.
In the lake, the clouds begin to calm.
There is a pattern to everything,
the way we rise, we fall;
the way I left the factories

seeking an education and left
the academy degreed
and still seeking.
The summer air soft.
Burnt tobacco
lingers around us
in fiery clouds.
When the water finally
settles, we all drift back
where we belong.

Three Songs for My Brother

I. Dive

At twelve, pliancy goes unnoticed,
the way the body spreads, skin
melds with the lake, head cutting
a wake for the body to follow.
He dives into the child-filled water
of Lake Elysian, the wooden dock
rocking with the motion
of too many adolescent feet.
He ignores the shock of cold,
holds his head under water
until he's out of air and then
breaks to the surface, gasping,
laughing at the chill.
He steps lightly on the sandy bottom,
following the dance he sees
all of the other swimmers make,
toes springing from the lake floor,
lithe as if gravity has flown.
He doesn't feel much at first.
His toe strikes something rubbery
so he pushes off of it;
steps onto a rock, but it's soft,
steps off of that onto sand.
It's a petty annoyance,
some intrusion in his path.
He pushes it with his toe
to see if it will just roll away,
and it does, but slowly;

as it moves, the bulk of the thing
shifts and when an arm
floats up and brushes his thigh,
he screams.

II. Levitate

It was only practice.
New Mexico and the girl there
with a name he couldn't pronounce,
the warnings from his Northern mother
that *those kind of people* never forget,
that they could come up
from the South with a sense
of revenge and ruin his bachelor's life.
In formation, everybody took a defused bomb,
ran the indicated distance
with bravado and adrenaline,
threw when the Sargent said throw.
By now, he was good at taking orders.
Vietnam was a promise rehearsed
like his two fiancees
one in the North, one in the South.
As he ran, he noticed only
the dry heat, the way the sand
kept giving out under his boots
with no water there to bind it.
The explosion was easy,
like jumping in the air

and the ground became a catapult;
it was only practice
moving toward heaven
with a half-severed arm
and the pain, not gravity,
pulling him back down.
Just before he blacked out.
he touched his lips to sand in greeting.

III. *Earthbound*

Bedroom walls draped
with thick velvet curtains
formed a soft black vault.
All summer long,
his reel-to-reel
from Vietnam
played *In-a-godda-davida*
or The Who's *Tommy*.
No one could see him.
No one could even stand the music.
Driving around town
in an orange Chevy ragtop,
his eyes betrayed
a perpetual haze
of beer and pot and sex;
he floated through
his parochial world
and wondered if
he'd left his body

back on the bombing range
or in that strangling jungle.
It was the sounds
that wouldn't go away,
bullets, explosions
cutting the air
in shrieks.
One mile faster
in the rusted car
and he was that much
farther away.
One more woman
in one more bed
and he was happy,
his body, briefly,
remembered.
One toke over the line,
Sweet Jesus,
one toke over the line,
and everything disappeared.

The Raspberry Wars

She didn't dare him to cut down
the stand of raspberries. Not really.

Just taunted him with *if you're man
enough* and he was. That fall

there was no raspberry jelly,
no cakes stained pink, no seeds

in the teeth. By the time I was ten
I could bake better than my mother.

She let the pie crusts go
when she saw my pastries,

their flaky light crusts in layers
like limestone shelves lining

the riverbanks nearby. Even I
played the game of defeating her

the pansy son who folded napkins
better than he threw a football

all fiery indignation in the kitchen,
beating batter by the spoonfuls

beating her, a beaten boy besting
someone, even my mother,

who only collected the raspberry
brambles as the old man cut them down

stood silently at the fence, remembering,
perhaps, as she fed the bushes

to the hungry fire, that there is
no redemption through pain.

Milarepa

With ears pressed to silver rails
we waited for our trains,
our fingers pressed on oiled rocks,

our faces set, summer air pausing,
like warm palms, over closed eyes,
sifting down collars of sweaty, worn shirts.

Always, it started with a dare.
With Sundays too big and holy,
with a boy's need to blaspheme.

Always, it started with vibrations.
With ears to the ground
and small pressures flowing

down polished iron, we breathed
through tight mouths,
faster and faster as the train approached.

And our voices, filled
with wish and dread,
could not be contained;

as the inaudible passed
into its aural realm
we started to sound in unison,

to sing in cracking soprano notes
the songs of the rhythm
of our thin, expanding universe.

from *This Brightness* (2007)

Prelude to the Afternoon of the Cats

Here, a bedroom in late afternoon, the dim gray light
of an approaching storm easing weakly through the window
of a small blue-gray house in a marginal neighborhood.

The gray light is glorious, if gray light can be glorious;
glorious the way light lives in Bierstadt's wistful visions
of the West; glorious in the way light plays across

the landscape of Ansel Adams' towering Yosemite.
Here, a man sitting on the bed, reading a tract that claims
academic work should be filled not with facts, but love.

The man is dubious. Having spent more than half his life
in school, studying what purported to be the cutting edge
wisdom of those days, he found no love in the Ivory Towers,

only systems of power, ethics delayed or destroyed by desire,
and a certain willingness to talk about but not act upon
any sense of empathy or compassion.

He stretches his long legs out and waits. The gray light
takes a certain amount of getting used to; reading
off-white pages, black texts, in poor light hurts his eyes.

He waits and soon the cats appear, one by one.
He's read that the ruins in Rome are filled
with the city's beloved strays, fifty thousand of them

filling the Colosseum, Apollo's temple, the Palatine Palace.
The cats are gray   *though not all cats are, not even in the dark*
and white and black. The man sits back and slowly

they climb onto his legs, demanding adoration.
The author of intellectual love will have to wait.
The cats have come again to roost and what can

the intellect say to that but *stop* or *take this offering as a gift.*
The man makes no attempt to move. What else is there to do
on such a day? A gray afternoon when he could be sleeping

but isn't? When he could be in a forest but instead
sits on a bed? When his mind has turned from higher matters
to higher matters still? The weight of the cats on his shins

and thighs; the urgency of their purring;
the way that love, in application, is stirring;
the way the gray light is glorious in its transitions.

Leslie and Sebastian

The summer light changes
after the Fourth of July,
she says while pushing
a stroller down a grand
street on the fifth.
Inside the stroller,
a baby boy who loves
the world, and whom
the world loves. His
white-blonde hair
catches the transformed
light as he watches
people loping by,
languid in summer's
heat. She must be
right. She sees things
clearly. The light plays
more dramatically now.
How sad, the cheat of
summer. One month
into the season and
our Northernness
robs us of it. This is
an evening of long
shadows. Soon, we'll
be in our gardens,
putting delicate things
to bed. The stroller casts
its mechanical shape
across the sidewalk.

In the heat, it's hard
to imagine winter, but
it's here in each of us.
In the way we throw
our bodies forward
into autumn. In the
way our shadows grow
stretched and thin.
In all of the edges
grown sharper with that
keen bright blade of light.

Kinderszenen (Scenes from Childhood)

One

There is never enough money. There is never enough to eat. When there is enough to eat, there is never enough of our mother because someone has to work. My father rarely works. My father works at being crazy. Being crazy is a lot of work. Being crazy requires money. There is never enough money. There's never enough to eat.

Two

I collect seeds in a jar. This is the year of the near foreclosure, the year of the second fake heart attack. My father grabs at his chest and rolls around on the floor. My sisters scream. I don't know about it, being with my brother down the street when it happens. The ambulance comes, sirens screaming. We wonder who died, then continue to play. My father convalesces. Being crazy is a lot of work; it takes practice to make your heart race. My father is fired from his job. My mother takes a job at a factory. The factory prints magazines and catalogs. My mother works the night shift. My father doesn't work at all. During the day, my mother does housework. At night, she makes catalogs and magazines. She never earns enough money. We never see her.

Three

We lose a piano. We lose some guns. We lose our minibikes. We lose our car. Things in this universe never vanish, but change, change form, change hands. Other hands now hold our things and we are going hungry. The bank asks for the house back. My mother panics. My father naps. Thinking we'll have to leave our house, I walk around the yard and collect seeds from each plant there. I put them in jars. I think I can plant them in whatever new house we move to. Someone else's house, maybe. A house stolen from other hands. When it becomes clear that we will not move, I take the jar of seeds and stow it in the crawl space under my bedroom floor. I leave it there. Years later, my mother moves to a smaller house. I forget the seeds.

Four

Our family cat is my best friend. I play with holly hocks, hide in tall grass in the big ditch along the highway. One day, two cars crash. Blood and glass everywhere. People flood the road. Police swarm. Onlookers trample our garden to get a better view. Through a shattered windshield, a man's face, trapped inside the car. His skull has taken a new shape. Sirens slice the summer air. Welders cut the cars apart but it's too slow a process. The face collapses. From my vantage point, I watch the man die.

Five

Steady breath. Steady breath. Steady breath. Pedaling up the hill near Rathaie's pasture. Pedaling past the cows. Crows perched on phone lines. The sun unbearable. My skin brown and burning. Steady breath. The scent of freshly cut alfalfa makes my mouth water. Remember the taste of honeysuckle juice, the taste of raw sweet corn stolen from neighboring fields. August's heat. The swamp drawn down by drought; the turtles resting in the sun; the dogs that chase from the lonely driveways of small farms. Steady breath. Pedaling. Getting somewhere.

Six

Another one gone. A ceremony in a small town, in a courthouse. A rare dress, my mother in tears and nice lady shoes. A cake. A keg. A drunken husband. A room now empty. A sister married. Another one gone.

Seven

Constant chatter from the canary my mother keeps because her mother always kept one. My grandmother's birds lived. My mother's die, one by one, small yellow corpses and a trip to the backyard where my best friend the cat lies buried. Add a canary. Plant a tree. My mother tries to live as she was taught. The cannas brought from Nebraska, from her mother's garden, grow bold and scatter around the garden in no particular order. Constant chatter from the canary as my father smokes in the dining room, the room where the bird's cage hangs. The chatter subsides in a gray smoky tide. My sister Linda coughs. The bird dies. The matches are struck, one by one. They flare. My father coughs.

Eight

I collect books. I steal books. I buy books. I borrow books. I bury myself in words.

Nine

We try to build a fort. My brother Andy cuts his hand on rusty tin. Blood everywhere. The fort is abandoned but the tin still stands, still nailed to a tree, thirty years later.

Ten

No one cries when he leaves. No one dies of heartbreak. I've seen this in the movies. He packs his things in plastic bags and goes off coughing in a powder blue Buick with power windows and power seats and lives at my sister Wanda's house, three and a half miles away. It seems like infinity, the distance we span. No one cries when he's gone. No one misses him.

Eleven

Across the chalk outline of my hand on the sidewalk, a small cat
stands. Brown. Dull. Crabby. He crosses the line. The one where I've
said *no*. He comes over anyway. We take him in.

Twelve

There is never enough money. There is never enough to eat. Nights,
I sit in my room and read. Days, I sleep through school, too tired to
read. Weekends, I drink or ride my bike

steady breath, steady breath, steady breath

always pedaling. My

cat Max sits on my lap. Always moving. Dreaming. A book open to
a particular page. A dictionary dealing out definitions. There is never
enough money. There is never enough to eat. I find I am always hun-
gry. I read in a book how it is accomplished. I look at a map. Then I get
ready to go there.

Thirteen

The night I find *Swan Lake* on television, the broadcast is grainy
on a black and white set. How he, the Prince, moves! How she, the
cursed Princess, dances! How can you believe in something you never
knew existed? The wonder of motion, arms as wings. How the wind
across the prairie tricks us into belief. How the soul conspires, at last,
to throw us into a world where we belong, to startle us awake, into
paradise.

The Brightness

      this brightness
though sun under clouds

molasses air

dulcimer notes clear
      sharp

small bells passing
through the spaces between leaves
      grasses

I don't know what stillness is

contrary voices arguing

magnolia's white blossoms
      fading

carpeting hard red earth

      this brightness
across acres of trees

verdant bushes blooming
      lurid

mountain crescent surrounding the camp
      with sharp pines

      rock spine

the accents here
      like the people
languid

a liquid language

tongues passing soft
      curled words
between one mouth and another

      this brightness

dulcimer wings

a song
      familiar in my bones

the way music speaks

a language remembered

forgotten as dreams
      half-buried

I can't say I could thrive here
      I could try

stay twenty years in one city
feet memorize streets
no need for directions

I don't know what stillness is

a winter road

                north

notes passing between trees

lights in houses
                small suns
dispel darkness

footprints in snow

                this brightness

across country

another climate

another time zone

North Carolina in spring

tulip poplar's waxy flowered wings
                scatter on the path

I don't know what stillness is

every bit of pollen on Lake Eden's face

wood bees

Scotch on the porch

friends I rarely see
        yet love

this brightness

stillness is   I know
        I don't know

someone told me

put a period

after every word

so you won't miss

the.

end.

of.

anything.

The Luminous Body

This is an ode to the belly.
This is a celebration of

all that once was concave;
the way shirts bagged out

from a thin waist,
an embarrassment of skinniness.

This is the belly of a man
at forty. A ponderous thing

that has never seen the inside
of a gym since high school.

A thing driven to expansion
by the betrayal of metabolism

and a sedentary life.
This is the story

of a shrinking and growing waist;
a collection of pants

in three sizes; the *should have*
gone on a diet; should have

joined the Y while they
were having that sale story.

This is the body in the mirror.
This is the body in the bathrobe.

This is the belly that confronts
when one sits up in bed,

round down there where
once it was flat.

This is not about bodies
on TV or film; not those

muscled sculptural marvels.
This must not be about

the guilt those beauties induce;
the way they entice, tug us

between the world of *I want
that* and *I want to be that*.

This is the story of the belly
of a man who looked away,

didn't see himself expand.
This is about age.

This is the way the body
moves, naked, down the hall

at dusk; the way fading light
plays over his new/old skin;

the way we learn to begin
again, in experienced bodies,

the ones that grow older
and cannot be stopped,

those we must learn to inhabit well,
those we must come to love.

The Spectral Body

You're just at that age, she says
when I say that three of my friends
have cancer. This, as a tiny camera

on the end of a scope flexes and
weaves its way through my colon.
The X-ray tells its story in light;

in luminous lumps; if black,
they read white; if malignant,
bright, bold, defiantly shining.

What age is that? I want to ask.
The one where we learn
all over again to say good-bye?

Three bald heads, glowing with
sweat; three wigs; the recognition
that the word *diagnosis* begins

with a grim sentence.
The colon on the screen
is a wondrous thing; is this

too proud a way to describe
such an organ? In folds,
in turns, it follows its

convoluted path. If I could,
I would paint such a thing;
amazing in its intricacy;

deadly in its propensity
to translate a life into a half-life,
a glowing isotope of *cure*.

I watch the camera's progress
as the doctor talks us through it.
He never says what he's looking for;

the source, I presume, of the pain
that's driven me to emergency rooms
in cities across the country.

One of my bald friends sleeps
all day. Another vomits in
the kitchen sink, determined

to make breakfast for her family.
The third fights the pain until
everything is eradicated;

only soul and eyes remain;
she glows golden in afternoon
sunlight. In the darkness,

I can see her moving from
room to room. On the monitor
the colon seems an elaborate thing;

all of the internal connections
clear in the camera's livid light.
But in the parking lot,

in the supermarket,
in the privacy of the bedroom,
it's harder to envision how

organ A connects to organ B;
to grasp what makes any of us live;
to feel the transformations

that signal impending disasters;
to know the light in our luminous bodies;
to see where that bright trouble lies.

Signs of Light

one

make the first mark in the dark, on a mountain
in secret, in a place no one can see

make the second mark in stone, at graveside,
knife's dull blade on granite

     in secret
     in a place no one can see

make the third mark in flesh
      knife's dull blade on granite
cut a line through skin, a line through bone

      make the third mark in flesh
fingers fly, spell across the body
      cut a line through skin
      a line through bone

two

scribble the words in their proper order
cast a spell
     fingers fly, spell across the body
make the mark of the saints
the mark of the beast

     scribble the words in their proper order
negotiate the signs of darkness, the signs of light

make the mark of the saints
the mark of the beast

the stone, like flesh, retains an impression
will not heal

trace symbols for darkness
symbols for light

the stones are scarred, lips traced across skin
the stones, earth's flesh, bear witness
will not heal

three

if it isn't enough, this light, this wind,
what will tie us to this earth?

if it isn't enough, cold shock of water
at the height of summer's heat
what will tie us to this earth?

if we run our hands across the table's rough top
at the height of summer's heat
will we feel it, the fragile, tactile connection to this world?

if we read in the hewn wood the silent grained words
will we feel it, the fragile, tactile
connection to this world?

around us, the mountains are speaking

and we read in hewn wood
the silent grained words

four

last night I fell asleep to the sound of wings
                    all around us, the mountains are speaking
and an owl flew past my window, singing a feathered song

                    last night I fell asleep to the sound of wings
I dreamed I turned into a bird
                    an owl flew past my window
                    singing a feathered song
and in the dream I understood everything

                    I dreamed I turned into a bird
the owl spoke the language of the mountains, the trees
                    in the dream
                    I understood everything

five

out across the dry lake bed a crow flies low
near rocks exposed when the water drained

we sit on the dock
                    near rocks exposed
the sun is high, the season burns

we stare at the dry lake bed, imagine it filled

103

all around us

       the season burns

and we dream ourselves across the world

we are here because we survived

       we dream ourselves
       across the world

    six

the summer burns and the body lies

       yet we are here
       because we survived

because of the hard will to live, to thrive

       and the summer burns
       and the body lies

yet we are here, watching a crow fly
black wash across blue sky

a word

    fly

       scribbled in air

a spell cast

       a hard will to live, to thrive

seven

we cross these mountains
                    old peaks
                            letters scribbled across sky

in the years it takes us to make this journey
the world writes itself across my face

we learn the treachery of the body

the body you once knew turns hard, grows strange
                    the world writes itself
                    across my face

the body I inhabit blames me, pulls me down
                    the body you once knew
                    turns hard, grows strange

    eight

hiking in the foothills, you find yourself lost
                    we learn the treachery
                    of the body
suddenly in thinner air, I find I cannot breathe

once familiar weight shifts from under you
                    I find I cannot breathe
so we sit, staring down at the camp

once familiar weight

shifts from under you

the body changes, familiar text erased

we sit staring down at the camp

a world we knew turns hard, grows strange

familiar text erased

we navigate a new terrain, try to map a route home

learn new paths

the treachery of the body

nine

the children in the corner house
have covered their lawn in paper flowers

a constellation of white tissue
across the night-dark grass

a word

star

scribbled in darkness

on a night like this, the stars cannot lie

the children in the corner house

have covered their lawn in paper flowers

the darkness can be bitter, but isn't

the stars cannot lie

the world is full of grace

a voice, two houses away, calls someone home
says something simple

a word

spell

spoken in darkness

says something about mountains, about stone,
a bird that passes too close to the moon and freezes

ten

all around us, the stars fly
the world is full of grace
and you and I on our way home

something simple
a map of the world known and unknown
a world covered in paper flowers

on this mountain top, the night's story:
wind speaks in tongues, birds translate
the world is full of grace

the first mark made in darkness, the second in stone

a word

        scar

spoken in darkness

a universe of paper flowers, a mountain found whole
                the third mark in flesh

a word I remember, a spell broken
                a world known
                and unknown

An Open Door

Across the sanctuary of a community church
a door stands ajar; stained glass windows
allow only some of the sun to enter; filtered
yellow, red, opalescent green drench the pews.
On the altar converted to stage, a circle of
students contemplates a question of vocation.
Through the open door, only light, daytime
invading the intimate dim familiar in churches,
the hazy quality of the house of god.
When a child, I wanted to be a vampire.
Or a scientist. Or an actor. The world
seemed open to me in a way it does not
seem open now. *What is your passion,*
the facilitator asks and students giggle.
What drives you? I try to focus
on the question at hand, but lose myself
in the sunlight streaming in through
the open door. In this, a sanctuary,
I don't feel safe. *What do you want
to be when you grow up?* Not a teacher,
certainly; not a soldier; not a poet.
Who lives in the gray corners of a church
besides mice? What is that face in
the stained glass? When in college,
I wanted to be an archaeologist, wanted
to dig into the storied dirt of time and
come up with some history. In this room
I want to be a priest. It could be comforting,
living in the dark spaces of a church,
just me and the mice. *What is your*

vocation, the facilitator asks and
at this moment, I'd say, I am
a bringer of light; a man who stands
in a doorway flooded by sun;
I am a bird; someone who learns,
in shadow, the real shape of brightness.

Excerpts from

Crossing Over, Crossing Back:
A Portrait of Marsden Hartley

One
The Art Lovers: New York, 1900

God is in the details, or the Devil is; whose hands are holding whose, and how those hands may build the sacred city of Whitman's comrades, the city of the Master's love. All morning in imaginary mountains, Marsden sketching vistas democratic, free of desire's dystopia. All evening with Winslow, Jamieson, Tweedy, with letters from Horace scattered about, blessings from the man who once kissed Whitman's lips and there was nothing profane in that, the way one comrade might love another, the way that love might arch like a bridge across an immeasurable America. Always, lessons in the morning. From Winslow's hands a palette pregnant with pigment, brushes whorled across paper and canvas until every possible scene is depicted, every unforeseen lover uncovered and imagined. At night, Marsden lies in his room, surrounded by his day's work, listening to the traffic and the crickets. And there, just under the sound of the cars and carriages on the street below, the whisper of Walt's breath, his words woven into the trees, his chant repeating

> *We two boys together clinging...*

Three
Songs of the Season: Maine, 1908-09

Even in summer the mountains, deep blue, are carved from ice. Marsden traces their shapes in sudden, small thrusts of paint until the patchwork of hills, trees, and lakes emerges from the canvas. In this way, he maps out his own world, renders

> *the God-spirit in the mountains*

and makes the paint sing

with the seasons: Winter's trees are heavy flags, evergreens groaning under their burden of snow. Marsden buries Maine in a blizzard, and silences, temporarily, the voices that urge him always to go, to keep on moving. Spring and summer, the blues are mellowed with orange and yellow and the sky is filled with clouds like white fire. Whitman's and Emerson's spirits haunt him, and Thoreau binds him to the earth as Autumn's birches grow rusty with age and begin to fade back into winter, their white trunks pale, like ghosts, slender, singing, whispering, filling the forest.

Four
Dark Mountain: North Lovell, Maine, October 1909

If the mountains possess a language, he cannot comprehend it. Even in summer's light, with solstice and the days that seem less to fade into night than into half-days, twilight and a faint memory of waking, the world seems dark. The paintings rise from the canvas in gradations of brown and black, the clouds sometimes white, but stained with the heaviness of the world's deep soil. It's the earth from which he cannot escape, the need to know the words the mountains speak, the trees speak, the constant chatter of waterfall and clattering leaves. The touch of grass must replace the touch of man,
    a big broad shoulder to brush by.
                 At night, when the light has grown too poor to paint, Marsden imagines eyes in the darkness, eyes in the trees, the earth's own structure as a lover sprung up from the sand to keep him company.
    Marsden, he whispers;
         Marsden, the leaves repeat;
             Marsden, says the grass.

As a night-hungry owl flies past, eying a vole which unwisely leaves its nest, the sound startles him, and for a moment, he imagines he feels the fingers of a lover, pressing hard against his chest.

Five
A German Officer: Berlin, October 7, 1914

Berlin's incessant parades are splendid and Karl is the soldier's name, he who knows everything about friendship and camaraderie. In his love of horses and soldiers and order, Marsden imagines Karl as commandant in white leather jodhpurs and a hat, white, enameled, and sharp. He cuts Karl across canvas with titanium white and mars black medallions, gives him a checkerboard of distinctions, dates, and letters; he makes him head of a white battalion, riding abstract into a strict ordered white Prussian heaven. Marsden has never yet succeeded in settling his love on the disorderly living, those men who tease him and then refuse to pose. Only when Karl is dead does Marsden realize that he loves him at all, and then vehemently.

Seven
Still Life with Eel: Bermuda, February 1917

The sun, for northern blood, is a sedative. Days, he lies on the beach, the warm Atlantic whispering to him every secret of rest. He finds he cannot sleep, but instead, works and walks in a stupor of half-waking. The scenery seems designed to make him horny, and Demuth does nothing to discourage this—Charles on his tour of Danish ships and blond sailors who will be bought, willingly, for a price. Marsden indulges until his brushes seem to conjure phalluses and orifices whenever they touch canvas. Cocks in palm trees, mouths in the waves, the tender flesh of a Marine's ass in the beach's rippling sand. It's more than Marsden can stand, as a man prone to savage hunger and the careful art of that hunger's suppression. His paintings are unspooled, and even the critics begin to comprehend the extent of his desires. After a month in lust's stupor, he finds himself beached on the hotel bed; Charles has gone out again to meet the fleet and hasn't been seen for days. Marsden lies on the sheets grown sweat-damp and prays for relief from his inertia. Through the window, upon whose sill rests a single white calla, he can glimpse the pale brown beach, the water there bluer than anything he could imagine or dare to paint. At the shore's edge, a lone sailor strolls, his thin Navy whites rolled to his knees, the fabric tight across his firm ass. Marsden suffers a momentary vision: a single eel, coiled around an amaranth; the vision is so sharp, so complete, it robs him of his breath. Tonight, finally, he will paint, even by lantern light. But today, he will go to the beach, where the lone sailor has stopped, and stands, looking up, his tanned arm raised as if in greeting, or recognition.

Eleven
Crossing Over, Crossing Back: Mexico City, Mexico, April 1932
Eight Bells Folly: Memorial to Hart Crane

Out of the shock of it, the anger, the sorrow, Marsden emerges, whole and howling, from the hungry sea. Not his body, but his personality, his presence on the canvas, so long lost in that flat, modernist desert. For this incarnation, his eyes are among the thirteen eyes watching as Hart dives to his death, the bells chiming eight times, high noon and a man driven back into the water from which he was born. Marsden feels he can never recover from this loss. Karl went charging to his death, but seeking glory, not obliteration. Hart sought madness in the ocean's depth, and found it. Hart sought not the bridge, but the water flowing below it, and found it. Now, Crane sleeps in the bosom of the sea, in the belly of the shark, in the arms of the waves which push this Cutty Sark back toward America. And Marsden imagines he stands at the ship's prow, his aging head covered in a thin black cloth, veiled in the style of the Mexican widows, wailing the way those women wail: loud, sharp, angry as if, in the power of their outrage, their voices could reach the dead, and carry them, swiftly, back to dry land, the world of the living.

Twelve
Mexican Mystical: Mexico City, Mexico, May 1932

"the one place I always shall think of as wrong for me"

Crane denied it, but Marsden knows that we can never escape from the world. When the telegram reaches him with the news of Hart's death, he shuts himself up in a small, dark library, and begins to search for answers. There is no peace under the water. Nothing to be found in the ocean or the ragged skin of Mexican mountains. Nature's caress is expensive, and calls us back to the elemental world with gestures plain as waves, the eruption of long dormant volcanos. The mystics offer only a temporary relief:
           Paracelsus
               meaning NOTHING,
                   the life-giving element in all things;
Rolle spread across the red clouds, his quest for transformation never complete, but always in that baited heat of
                   becoming.
                      In the end, Marsden is

still unsatisfied. The Mexican men who pass by the walls of the library know someone is watching them through the ancient, clouded glass—that crazy, tall American who cannot speak Spanish, but whose eyes burn like lanterns day and night. They've seen this before, and so walk on, leaving the painter alone with his books, his hot looks, his vague desire for the things of this world and the next.

Fourteen
Fisherman's Last Supper: Nova Scotia, November 1936

His boys wed their lover, the sea, although Alty said he loved Marsden, and meant it in the way a young man means it: the words currency enough with which to purchase the last of a life's contentment. Old men have hearts which crave more, but require less than the young, so it was enough: Alty's promise that one day he'd build a house for himself and Marsden to live in, just the two of them, near the water. When the storm blew in, he had no premonition, not the way he expected love would be, full of prescience and foreboding. The waves said nothing and Marsden slept as he always slept near the sea: calm, restful. In the morning, the mother told him everything, the way mothers have for centuries reported the deaths of their sons to others: with the containment of one who has been emptied, and still, fears there is something left to lose, and something else to protect. When he heard, Marsden screamed until a small bone in his throat snapped and taught him, beyond language, what severance is. The next morning, he fled, again by water. As he left the island, he kept his jealous eyes shut, unable to look down at the face of the full, contented sea.

Sixteen
Madawaska: Acadian Light-Heavy
Bangor, Maine, 1939

The light is painted to fall from the left, and the model's nipples shine
with a radiance which begs that they be licked. Marsden lies in his
letters:

ave no interest in the subject matter of a
picture, not the slightest,

and finally, no one believes him. What he captures
on the canvas is the essence of what, in bodies, makes us *hungry*, makes
us want to eat the lover above *and* below the skin, to get into the bones
themselves and live there in a passion always and never satisfied. The
boxing trunks, Marsden darkens down, aware that what is not shown
begs expression, props desire up one step further on a ladder of pan-
icked invention. As the paint dries, he tests the oil each day with the
edge of his thumbnail; once across the broad brown shoulders; once
across the stomach which vanishes into the waistband of the deep blue
trunks; once across the illuminated neck, thick and hot with bright
yellow pigment; once across the nipples flat and red, burning like twin
stars on the young man's chest.

Seventeen
Dead Plover, with Ribbons: Corea, Maine, 1940

Coaxing the black bird with his brush, Marsden wakes the plover with
oily strokes, though the bird is dead, another visitor from surf and sea,
brought down by the hard demands of dry land. He gives the dead
thing ribbons because something must be regal in this picture: a simple
bird; a weathered board, wave-washed; the texture of sand, water, earth.

119

This is the way he remembers old women in mourning when he was a boy: black silk rustling past half-open doors, faces hidden behind dark lacy veils, the scent of roses and rotted longing. And ribbons, festive as a fair but somber, as if death itself were a reason to celebrate. As it could be, for those long married, long suffering under the tutelage of a harsh husband's hand. Marsden is like those old women now. His face grown heavy, jowls hanging so Lipchitz sculpts them like the flanks of an aging mare: soft, flaccid, flowing toward earth. Everything at this age drags him down, closer to the land that he's painted all of his life. The plover rests, quiet messenger from the land of contentment, a land whose location has eluded Marsden his whole life. Something in the rustle of black mourning dress, a whispered secret in the stress of silk against silk against silk, a pale hand, jeweled with moonstone and lapis, copper and tourmaline. Marsden thinks that if he can paint the bird just so, the secret of death's slow sleep will be revealed. He paints the bird once, with ribbons. Again, with a mate also drawn from death's wake. But no. Nothing comes from the bird's empty beak, no song, no call, no notion of what constitutes rest, no lessons in immortality.

Nineteen
A Rooftop Restaurant, Sunset: New York, NY, 1943

Finally, he is able to pay the check. Running into Adelaide on the city's burgeoning streets, he admires the color of her young son's eyes and invites them to dine with him, in elegance, on the roof of a good hotel. He's made sales, finally; found a dealer, finally, who deals in paintings, not charity. He recalls every begging letter to Stieglitz:
    Dear Alfred, I'm cold and the rent is due.
    Could you advance me something so I can eat?
Always, a check with admonitions to return to America, become an

'American Painter. But how could he? Geography means more than national boundaries and the heart settles where it senses the safety of home. Always, he has been denied this. Always, he has been and made himself alone. Hard to change, at sixty-eight, the habits which have protected a lifetime. But finally, he stops in America, in New York, the anonymity of raging streets and immigrants and wars; Europe was Matisse and Klee and Stein, who once said he was the best American painter, then changed her mind, then died. Now he tries to remember the color of her eyes, but cannot. Perhaps they are like the boy's eyes, like Adelaide's, who sits across from him and looks at him like a daughter at a father whom she has lost, then found. He imagines, to himself, his fellow diners perhaps mistake this woman and child for his own family, of whom he is proud: a daughter, or a wife, a child who resembles his own younger self. This is a new age, where he can paint, and sell, without worry; where he can live in a good hotel and travel if he likes, if he still requires that sanctuary of another country. The sun is setting. Adelaide squints and tries to recall when she's seen him this happy, Marsden the old man, Marsden the daddy of birds and rocks and mountains. He knows she is watching him, recording. He is looking at the sunlight as it fades across the buildings, stealing details he can paint in later. He feels quiet, rested. He hopes she will not forget, hopes she will write all this down: how Marsden is content; how the young boy in the sunset is beautiful; how there is nothing more to wish for; nothing more to want.

Twenty-one
First Light; Ellsworth, Maine, September 2, 1943

He wakes well at dawn, though the sky, dull red, gives warning. Through a slight part in the curtains he sees the sun just emerging, a glowing crack in the world's dark face, a rhapsody of opposites. Things lately are changed by a clarity Marsden hasn't known, or maybe knew as a speechless child. He feels he's returning to a way of seeing that he can only describe as *sewn*. The whole world is stitched together. The sky, in reds and blues, is stitched. The tree tops he can see from the hospital window, green stitched to darkness stitched to fading blue. His hands, pale and pink, held up against the bed sheets, starched white, stitched to the fabric. He longs to paint, now that he knows how the world goes, how its elements fit together. Everything is in pieces: darkness and light; love and hatred; joy and sorrow; color and monochrome; fullness and hunger; cold and heat; longing and fulfillment; blindness and sight, sweet, sweet sight. Everything is in pieces. All he can do is try to stitch the broken world back together.

from *Sin Eater* (2010)

Two Children Menaced By A Nightingale

after Max Ernst

I'd wanted only a beautiful house, but it wasn't so.
A crack in the ceiling's plaster a rift,
a great cleaving, one room into two.

Down the street, a small boy and girl rolled
an old tire. They shrieked each time
the tire fell, spinning round and round like

a dime on a table top, each cycle bringing
that roundness closer to the earth.
This was the way in my neighborhood.

Cars passing, rattling with music.
Freeway traffic too distant to witness, yet,
always that low, merciless din.

Nothing came about quite as I liked.
Accidents advance most of our lives and
this realization made me bitter.

The whole house shook in anger some days.
I felt myself dwindling. The children and
the tires and the cars and the birds all

seemed to caterwaul at once. It was chaos.
I couldn't sleep nights, and days,
I longed only to sleep. All the while,

he was there, disapproving, collecting,
filling our fraying house with so many
things that the wooden beams, ancient

and long, sang without end.
I wanted to escape, but lacked a plan.
In the country where I was born,

mourning doves and purple finches
named the daylight.
Owls and nightingales, the darkness.

Easter *(ending on a line from Apollinaire)*

By midday the wind has come
to blow away the promised storm

so I sit in the backyard, watch
bits of yellow pollen collect

on my blue flannel shirt;
it seemed so slight when I picked

it out in the morning's gray, now
too heavy in the sunlight.

He always called these "progress winds."
That's what must have blown against us

all of our years together, blew through us
in the end, as if we were paper ghosts.

Today I see his name in the local news.
What progress has he made since we separated?

What progress have I made since I left him?
I've never told all those I should that I love them.

I cannot account for the things I have done.
I praise all those who love me.

Clara's Vision (Appalachian Trail)

We drove for hours across terrain
I couldn't recognize; through
small towns that read:
church, church, feed store, church.
We arrived near sunset,
when the light was gently capping
each ridge, cutting the edges
of rocks in red, pink, gray.
I didn't know what heaven was,
but perhaps this was it:
clouds sweeping gravel paths;
granite disappearing, then reappearing,
in the mist; small peaks poking out of
miniature white mountains within mountains.
The air was thin. I thought I might faint.
You pointed along the serpentine path
and told me it went all the way
up to Canada. How far was that?
How many lifetimes would it take
to traverse that distance? Since I'd met you,
I'd only wondered, more and more,
how one can come to be saved,
I mean truly saved, not the
down-on-your-knees, begging
to be forgiven saved, but the kind
where we each come to know ourselves
-radiance and repulsion aside-
just simply to know ourselves.
I thought you'd found that
and I wanted it too.

As the sun set, the path began
to fade into an impenetrable darkness.
You said we'd hike the whole trail
one day and I believed you.
Then, back to the truck
for the long ride home.
I didn't know then what heaven was,
but I wanted to believe you did.

Three Gifts

I want to tell you of the curve of space,
the roundness of time, but life intrudes.
Instead, I'll tell you of the roundness
of the melons at the grocery store,
overpriced and out of season;
of the thumb thump as I strike each one
to find the ripest of what, in this month,
should not be ripe at all.

I want to compose for you a treatise on the soul,
the transmigration of spirits, our infinite lives.
Instead, I'll give you a singular schedule
that's fixed every day; the way the house
sounds and smells at dawn; the quietness
of an early spring street when no one is out
walking a dog or cutting the grass.

I wish to hand you, at last, my heart,
my true heart, and not on my sleeve,
not on a platter or the end of a spear,
but in my hands, a red, still-beating gift,
proof of all I've ever said and done
in the name of love. Instead, I'll show you
one last scene, too domestic to be of use,
but true in its composition:

I'm standing at the kitchen sink
at five p.m. washing dishes.
I'm thinking of nothing, really;
half looking out the window,

half watching as the soap suds
curl down the drain. And I'm waiting,
always, at that singular hour,
the one in which you leave your office,
get in your car, and begin the journey home.

The Soul in Paradise (I)

My particular paradise is solitude, so
pray let me find a room with no windows,
no doors; a chair with three legs;
a telephone without a cord.
Let me find a table laden
with the Holy Leftovers of the Last Supper,
Christ's cup tipped, a few drops of wine
left to lick from the thick, coarse table top,
some bread, some salt, a vinegar-soaked rag.

He thinks I want to be a martyr, but I don't.
He thinks there must be a system of rewards
and punishments, where one earns the right
to suffer. But there's not. The angels here
aren't terrifying, only angry. They can't
have souls so they beat us up
with their sharp wings, throw us off
the tops of clouds and skyscrapers.
They watch us scream all the way down
and when we recover, they start again.
In my paradise, everything is equal
but nothing's fair. We're cursed
to count every shade of white.
In my paradise, *chaos* isn't a dirty word.
He may try to get there, but he can't.

I've learned the trick of starving myself
until my body's so thin it can pass
through a wall's molecules.
This is something he cannot learn.

Inside my room, utterly silent,
I'll come to know nothing.
This will take me years.
He'll pound and pound on the walls
but I'll hear nothing. Only the ruffle
of sinister angel wings, and
the sound of my blood as it rushes
through my heart, my hands, my head.

Three Fairy Tales

One

He walked away and didn't come back. That's how it was. If I'm going to be completely honest, I have no better story to tell. It was twilight. It was December and bitterly cold. My stomach ached with it, that kind of loss for which I have no name other than pain. For days after, I looked out the picture window, hoping to see him limping up the walk, or standing in front of the house across the street. I made up all kinds of scenarios to address what I didn't know. I knew nothing. I knew he had been here, and now was gone. I knew I'd done nothing to help him, nothing to stop his going, and now I was afraid.

Two

You'll want to pay attention to this one. It's about a small girl who gets lost. She suffers a series of misadventures along the way, none of them pleasurable or instructive, none of them even cautionary; that's the way it is sometimes, bad circumstances that are pointless, irredeemable, useless except as a means to make us feel lucky for what we have or guilty for what we have not suffered. Her story is thus: she was born. She belonged to someone, had a home. Then, there was turmoil, a sudden need to flee. She was lost along the way and never found the path back. Now she lives in a hovel. People feed her scraps and, maybe, give her warm water on the coldest days. I can't say honestly if she dreams of something better; perhaps she's forgotten all of that, and perhaps that's best. She eats and sleeps and looks out over the yard she's come to call home.

Three

We could start with his birth. That's a certainty. And with his heart.
He had one. Good or bad, no one can say, because he was plagued
by spirits all of his life; bad spirits or good; when one comes into the
world, it's shadow travels along, just to keep the universe in order. Per-
haps his childhood was difficult. In those days, that was the usual case.
And at some crucial point, that place in one's life when one makes
that leap from child to man, he fumbled. He killed those he loved.
Bad spirits traveled with him after that; good spirits as well, though
their mouths were sutured shut with all the ill he had done. He came
to walk only in the night, sometimes like a man and sometimes like
a beast, sometimes like a bird, sometimes like a snake. The spirits still
travel by his side; the bad worn thin as bird's bones; the good so filled
with all they cannot say that they threaten to burst at the first gentle
gesture a human hand might make.

First Morning

Wind shakes the small house
where, all night, I sleep, then wake,
to the basso foghorn's desolate call,
to the circling cry of coyotes.
I cannot guess how near they come
to the thin-walled house;
close enough to blow it down?
Hard to rest in stillness when
I'm used to rigged-up cars, their music
shaking the neighborhood.
Bass of the foghorn,
bass of the beat;
any sound a lullaby
if it rocks you to sleep.
Here, a constant chattering
of birds and the sharp scent
of wild fennel growing
just outside the door.
Down the hill, the beach.
the Sound
with its changing tides.
It's difficult to navigate
in any new geography,
difficult to breathe
in the salt laden air.
What looks like a cloud
in the distance is a mountain,
and I've never seen such trees,
tall as buildings, more ancient
than the city in which I live.

Here, the roads wind, take longer,
and I can't say where they go.
The water, from my cabin door,
sequins shimmering
through fog-filtered sun.
If I walk out, just steps
from my tiny porch, I could
roll, slowly, down
the dry brown hillside,
toward the foghorn's
call, that gasping sound.

If You Call

I'll tell you how the pine trees
look from here: silhouettes against

silver water; black; jagged; bent
in centuries of invisible wind.

I'll tell you how the houses
have weathered storms, their

clapboards a patina of white
and gray; of the startling green

of doorways and window frames;
how one, with a turret, resembles

a castle lost in the new world.
I'll tell you how autumn feels here;

how the wind carries in it something
of winter; how alone it seems some days;

how new, and thrilling, others.
I'll tell you how I think I could learn

to call such a place home, whether
with or without you. This will sound

hard, though it isn't meant to be.
Some of us are better off alone, apart

but close enough to touch or hear.
I'll tell you how it comforts

to listen to the voices of strangers
passing on the path below.

Lullaby

Back home, he coaxes
each of the cats

onto the bed before
he sleeps.

Together, they wrap
themselves around

him, form a blanket
where my body

used to be.
Here, I pile

layer after layer
of quilts across

the bed, use their
weight to pretend

that everything's
the same.

Pacific houses
are never

warm enough.
I leave lights on

while I sleep.
The coyotes,

on the hillsides,
call in hunger

to one another
all night long.

Long Distance

Four hundred miles away his mother is dying,
so he's gone home to see her for the first

and last time in twenty years.
He calls to say she's a tough

old bird, but her breathing's labored.
The peonies in the bed outside

bloom with deep pink outrage.
He's been tending the garden this year.

All that he plants seems to thrive.
The spring's been wet and so all that's alive

is larger than life, fantastic flowers, threatening vines.
When he called again this morning to say

she's holding on, I wanted to tell him:
sometimes the dying stay with us,

in fear or devotion, until we convince them
it's time to move on, and then they let go.

Figure in White

She comes walking
down the narrow path
toward me. Her long,
white woolen cape
spreads out in her wake,
a cloud of light pulling
the afternoon along.
Beyond her, the sky speaks
of nothing but rain.
The ocean, gray
with lapses of whitecaps,
has spilled into the sky
so I can't say anymore
where water ends, sky begins.
As she nears me
I can see she's smiling.
This could be for me.
It could be for no one.
She simply smiles.
The path is easy.
It's downhill for her.
Perhaps momentum
brings pleasure.
I smile back as she passes,
she nods gently.
Behind, as I push
myself up the hill,
I can hear the clack-clack
of her shoes as she moves
swiftly away.

Figure in Red

In proportion to the mountain
she is small, a red sliver measured
against the side of a white house.
Across the Sound, the edge of
a town abandoned at the turn
of the last century, then picked up
again in this one; its old function,
shipping; nostalgia, its new.
She moves with precision,
hands deep in pockets,
hair under a cap or bundled
atop her head. The fog drifts
from the edge of the lawn
to the meadow beyond.
She flows with it, smooth, quick.
In a moment, she's gone,
a village vanished in the fog.

Figures in Silhouette

There are three of them,
black against the water's
blinding backlight,
all that glittering.
They stand near the edge
of the cliff. They're talking.
Their words, animated
as the sea, are flowing
back at me in my cabin,
perched on the side
of the hill. Near them,
a car with trunk and doors
open. I see a long journey,
departure or arrival
uncertain, only, in the cadence
of their speech, in the way
they touch one another
on the sleeve, a sense
of urgency, of connection.

A Constellation

The room was full of stars.
Their light white, iridescent.

The blue behind them, darker
than my darkest dream.

He was there. He wore
a shirt embroidered with stars.

Against that night sky,
I could barely see him.

I thought it better to stay,
discontent as I was.

As I woke, he threw
the window open.

The vacuum was broken.
All of the stars rushed out.

The Temple of Dendur

Of the structure itself, I recall very little.
Taken apart there, stone by stone,
reconstructed here, in this great glass hall,
whose wall of windows looks out on a park
and a street full of people and buildings
and cars unimaginable when this temple
was first raised. Of the day,
there's the blur of a first, belated trip
to New York, itself as much a myth
as the pyramids to a man,
raised as I was, in a landlocked state
in the middle of a country that's
barely conscious, if seen in
the scope of a global history.
Of the light that poured in through the mass
of windows, there's much to be said;
how it struck Carla's hair,
played across the pale golden strands;
how it turned my sun-deprived skin
a healthy tan; how it coaxed something
of the ancient desert from mid-March streets.
Of the city itself, the crowds that
engulfed us, I can say it seemed
that everything and nothing was possible
that day. Winter was holding us,
though daffodils bloomed in the park
outside. Carriages sauntered along
streets next to buses and trucks.
I felt both lost and found,
sitting in a temple that was, itself,

an immigrant. I was visiting
a friend I'd known for twenty years.
This city was now her home.
We were talking as though
no time had passed, as though
we knew one another's secrets
still, though it had, and we didn't,
and never would again.

Winter Vigil

Something, a dozen yards from the house,
waits in the snow. Dusk settles early.

To resuscitate the day we install floodlights,
print a permanent dawn across darkness.

On the other side of the yard, at the edge of
this new brightness, it turns again, lopes off

into a blankness at the edge of the light's plain.
Something waits, still and deep and ancient.

The rest of my family, asleep
in early winter beds, in dreams

of spring, are engulfed in an orderly
procession away from this envelope of hunger,

of cold. I'm alone with it. I can see its fur
glisten in the moonlight. The line between

outside and inside stretches impossibly thin.
In a few hours, the rest will wake.

Daylight will drown out the darkness.
January's monsters will melt like the snow

through which we now swim.
This one deep in fear. This one crouching.

Encounter, Late

startled by the beauty of its form

headlights illuminating asphalt

only
a second
then the buck
framed perfectly
delivered
from darkness into this moment

frozen
midair

our eyes meet
creature to creature

we both know what's to come

shattering glass and metal torn
and I'm screaming louder
than I ever have before

the car's body stops but
my body's still moving
the dashboard
the window
yanked back by the seat belt

he continues his flight
back into the void

I crawl from the totaled car
run breathlessly a mile up the hill
to my home

        the stars are cold
and hard
      and the night air sharp

in the ditch he finds a way
out of this world's darkness

Wrapped (Red)

Weakened gulls plunge into the sea;
       seals drift with the current, wash up on the beach.
          Animals crawl into the quiet dark.

Where do we go, you and I?
       Heaven's been
          destroyed for each of us.

Hummingbirds abruptly stop.
       The one you found in the meadow
          last week

seemed to have materialized
       midair, then fell like a stone.
          You wrapped him in red thread,

as you'd seen Mexican women do
       in the casting of spells.
          You placed him on a calla leaf,

left him to his own.
       Now we go our separate ways.
          Reunion has no guarantee.

We carry that knowledge every time we part.
       Such simplicity, transcendence.
          Someone must be there

to pray for our peace,
       gently close our eyes,
          unspool a length of thread.

Sin Eater

I'd grown fat with it, like most do.
Every day the receptacle of all
that rage, anguish, that madness.
Not everyone is made for listening;
priests, perhaps, in the confessional;
psychologists and their couches;
those like me who feel we
must stay and take it in.
An ancient Welsh tradition
allows a family to hire a Sin Eater
when a loved one dies.
The Sin Eater comes and devours
the feast the family has placed
around the corpse.
With each morsel of food,
the Sin Eater takes into himself
the missteps of the dead;
when the table is cleared,
the dead one goes to heaven
and the Sin Eater goes mad,
filled as he is with
someone else's sorrows.
For months, I feasted at his table.
I'd lost all sense of hunger or satiety.
My mouth remained open
and his miseries flew in
bite by bite by bite.
Even now I recognize the effect:
When I spot a table
laden with food,
I back away.

Devil's Work

Forty-one was a desperate year—
addictions and deletions:

the year I struck that match and
burned down my own house.

I should have known—
sowing fire in my own bed—

nothing survived.
Now I have nowhere to go.

Spring came and I was ready
to fly, but the pilot said no,

the craft wasn't airworthy.
I begged and was met with

silence. That year, none of
the bulbs I'd assiduously

planted came up. Blight
in my garden. Everywhere

I went, I saw wings.
Little redheaded birds

took over our blue porch.
I didn't know their names

so I called them harbingers
of doom. I was desperate.

I'd have tried anything.
It gets that way in the dark

years, those our parents
cannot warn us about

because, when we're born,
when we're young, they're

living through them. So many,
then, come undone;

houses burned, birds in flight.
My own did. And now me.

God's Monkey

Amidst that flying hoard, all chattering,
feathers, and fur, one of them must have
had good intentions. The one who swooped
down to catch the dog, then dropped him,
providing a momentary chance for escape.
Another dove to take his place and the girl
and her dog were captured, to be rescued later.
I depend on cavalry or angels.
The boy who notices, while walking
among the ruins of a tsunami-wracked town
that something small, dirty and in with the debris
that once was a home is moving, waving, even.
A child's hand. Small miracle.
For decades after their execution, some scholars
believed that one Romanov had survived,
What would that princess be like now,
a century later? Impossibly old.
There's no one left to tell this story, save
what scientists may reconstruct from bones
salvaged from an abandoned well.
I need one voice to tell how it really happened.
With Roanoke, only a word carved into a tree:
Croatoan. No campsites. No bodies. No secret
journal. Visitors there swear they see women
at chores, children at play, men cleaning muskets.
Waiting for their stories to finally come to light,
if in fragmented details:
Virginia Moore, infant, passed in the night;
Thomas Kent, drowned while fishing;
Joshua Cooper and family, vanished;

Mistress Browne, disappeared at the well;
Sally Thomas, fallen from cliff;
Seth Browne, infant, carried off by a winged creature.

The Soul in Hell (I)

I want a system of checks and balances,
a careful tally, an affidavit of authenticity.
I want a lake of fire through which to swim.
I want everything I own stacked into
a funeral pyre, a stone for my head.
I want eternal summer,
no autumn, no winter, no spring.
I want a world devoid of transitions.
A television that receives a single transmission
of game shows and talk shows and cartoons.
I want to own the secret of everything.
I want to sit in the Ark on frozen Ararat
and meet the Yeti. I want to know
what the cat says, what the bird sings.
I want to translate the leaves of grass
from English back into tongues.
I want super powers.
I want night vision.
To stare into the sun and never go blind.
I want to know the monsters in the closet.
I want to kiss the prince upon
his sweet pink ass and have him
turn back into a toad. I want eternal life.
I want to die and rise again.
To cook the fish and eat all the loaves.
I want to make love to the Seven Deadly Sins.
Knock every terrifying angel off
the heads of their heavenly pins.
Spin a camel into thread
and pass it through the needle's eye.

I want to ride Leviathan down
to his frigid, watery bed.
I want to dance perfectly, speak
perfectly, eat and shit and curse perfectly.
I want world peace and domination.
I want a hundred soldiers in my bed.
I want to stop the world as it spins.
To stretch my hungry lips up to kiss
the drowsy old face of God.

The Soul in Hell (II)

Die Ordnung der Engel

They come, at last, to take me. I've done my best
to hide but they see through my human disguise.
We face a long set of stairs. I walk slow, deliberate,
like a man on his way to the gallows.
It seems there is no hell, only what the mind creates,
and my imagination is tired. It's all that's been
holding them back. At the top of the stairs
is a plane we'll board, so quiet and orderly—
I'd tried to board it once before but was turned away—
the seats are assigned. Every angel has one.
Mine is at the back, close to the toilets, away
from the heavenly hosts. I must board last
but I've nothing left to check, no bag
for the overhead bin. Our belief in gravity
holds us to the ground, but here, the rules
don't apply. I strap myself in so I won't float away.
The propeller starts to spin. The pilot says
it's time. I brace myself for takeoff.
The horizon is endless once we're in the air,
like it was when I was a boy staring out into
immeasurable fields. How small I felt then, sure
I could never cross such a distance.
Now I move on to new territories, fields
of perfect rows that cross-hatch one another
forever. Such a strange word: forever.
Like a gift or a curse. A promise made to
a frightened child when he asks his mother,
how long will I live?

from *Two Men Rowing Madly Toward Infinity* (2016)

35 South

Craning my neck to see the hawk
you just spotted on the telephone wire,

I see only low hills and fields.
After thirty years this land is invisible

to me, the route, pure habit.
I know things change.

The lanes shift, a house grows up
in the maple woods where, each spring,

green buckets were tied to the trunks
of the trees. My blindness is learned,

willful. If I don't see my world
slowly turning in on itself, then

that hawk will never catch the rabbit
that hides in the weeds.

I will never turn into the man
I don't want to become.

The Crows

The hollow field, stripped of cornstalks,
is carpeted by dozens of them. When a car passes,
they all take flight at once, a black cloud against
October's sharp blue sky. I'm told they have
two languages. One, the familiar social call,
the caw-caw announcing: I am here.
The other is quieter. A low chirping spoken
only in a family nest, nothing meant for outsiders.

I ride the elevators with my sister, who is dying
and needs new lungs. The hospital is enormous,
a hollow concrete box that towers dozens of stories
into the sky, burrows dozens of stories below.
We travel from floor to floor, lab to lab, doctor to doctor.
Everyone measures something but no one makes
any promises. In this, they are all very precise.

When a crow dies, others will gather for a vigil
in the trees. No language here, only silent
observation, a voiceless wake. When it's time,
each bird knows to fly off alone.

My sister doesn't say anything after the last appointment,
just finds me in the waiting room and says, *let's go home*.
The list, it seems, is not for her. The line for a new set
of lungs is long, and her body is starved for oxygen.
We don't speak on the drive back to Saint Paul.

A murder of crows. Such a menacing name
for these intelligent birds. Studies show they possess

long-term memory, are intelligent as a three-year-old.
When I was a boy, a neighbor kept one as a pet.
It loved shiny things, would fly down to snatch
a foil gum wrapper or a lost ring, anything that
glinted in the sun, caught the light, became radiant.

We sit, silent, in the living room as the television
rambles and my cats seek out the last daylight.
Silence is the secret language in our family, the long gaps
between what we can and cannot say. She dozes under
a heavy quilt as I stare out the picture window,
then get up slowly, and quietly walk away.

Horses in Snow

Fading dusk turns the snow into stars,
the sky and the horizon line into
a black dome. The only world I know
exists in the twin beams of my headlights.
I'd forgotten what it's like, driving
a country road in a blizzard, the way
the wind swirls the snow across the road
in eddies, like water on a troubled lake.
I'd forgotten the hypnotic effect
of the flakes flying at the windshield,
how my eyes try to focus on each flake,
lose sight of the road itself.
I've never been afraid of night
in the city, but night in the country,
the storm enveloping everything,
makes all of the folktales
true, all of the cautionary monsters
stalk the forest that fences in
the freeway. I become a child
behind the wheel, a boy sent on
a man's errand because there is no one else.
I drive slowly from village to village,
seeking out the safety that will not
be found. When the tires hit a patch
of ice, I'm pulled back into myself,
back into the doubled view of
the headlamps, and as the car reaches
the top of a rise, its lights shine
into a bend in the road, a pasture beyond.
There, for a moment, stand dozens

of horses. Some are unmoving under
blankets of snow. Some are feeding
from hay-filled troughs. And one
is galloping, moving fast as me,
head down, trying to outrun the storm.

Portrait of Viola

They lived without electricity.
Their water came from a hand pump
at the base of the windmill.
A Nebraska farm, 1935.
She said, *you can't miss what you
never had.* Drugstore goldfish
in the water tank turned into
giant orange and white carp,
Koi prized in another country,
another class. Her father threw them
out into the prairie claiming
they'd poison the cattle.
Rattlesnakes, a way of life,
careful checking before eggs
were gathered from the darkness
of nesting boxes. Everywhere, heat.
Gone with the Wind
in 1939. She was fourteen.
During the war, she looked like
one of the Andrews Sisters.
First child at twenty, last at thirty-nine.
All survived save one, gone
at thirty. The death of her daughter
turned her hair white.
Eighty-four and she's lived alone
for longer than she was married,
her husband a man with a wild imagination
but a weak mind. He was born
the year the Titanic sank.
That should have told me something.

Now, central air for the worst
of the heat. In her lifetime:
organ transplants, space flight,
television, artificial hearts.
On still nights she sleeps with
just a sheet, the window open wide,
summer's heat as hard and dry.

Midwest Landscape: Empty Farm

Stunning, the red barn in decay,
gaps in the walls allow the sun's rays
to penetrate the building, bisect it
with light. We used to play there,
in the hay loft, tumbling across
the rectangular bales, diving into
piles of loose straw, dangerously close
to the open trap door, the ladder
upon which we came and went.
The family that lived here has scattered.
Some are dead. Some married and
one, a girl my age, was widowed young
when her husband contracted AIDS.
No one thinks about that anymore.
Students who are less than half my age
don't know anyone who is sick,
no one who has died. It was the plague
that ruined my youth. The farmhouse,
like the barn, is failing.
The landscape is dotted with spaces
like these, empty places where it seems
the families simply changed their minds.
Got up one day and left.
Ghost ships on the prairie.

No Love Lost

In the country, where the night is night
and no moon means no vision, the light

that pollutes the cities, robs their skies
of stars, is almost powerless. Walk down

the gravel road and see each oasis;
illuminated farmsteads scattered

across the prairie. Yard lights, flood lights,
barn lights that burn all night

as one animal struggles to give birth
to another. I lie down in a grass field

still spring-soft, dazzled by the face
of our spiraling galaxy. Unable to name

any constellation, I remember:
I was never drawn to the stars.

That was another boy who left me
behind in another life three decades ago.

What is time in the lives of the stars?
Maybe I was never here, and neither was he,

and no love existed between us.

A Trip Down Market Street
    April 1906 / March 1987

The Miles Brothers mount a camera
to the front of a cable car. The water
on the street tells us this is spring.
Everyone wears a proper hat.
The newsboys are astounded by
the contraption. They run in circles
around the car as it turns at the end
of the line. The tarp flap that covers
the back of a horse-drawn wagon
lifts and a small boy looks directly
at the lens, then returns to his canvas
covered dark. In a few days, these buildings
will fall and burn. These people will be ghosts.

The first time I saw San Francisco, it was
already a city of spirits. 1987. The age of AIDS.
Men on the streets were thin, aged decades
in a month, had fierce, burning eyes.
I had never felt so frightened or so free.
The streets pulsed with possibility.
None of my friends had yet died, and
all of us were dizzy after the long
Midwestern winters, the stifled lives,
the grim, Germanic facades. What could
any of us do but go wild? This was a city
that seemed to say *yes* to everything.

There was a wonderment of bodies
with flesh that had never known the cold.
Our hearts thawed. Everywhere, plants

bloomed in the sidewalk cracks.
Rich and Ruth had a lemon tree
in their garden and some days, it was enough
to sit under it, drink in the exquisite scent
of the blossoms. I wore the gentle fog
like a cape. I pulled it around me.
I turned like a dancer and watched it swirl
and grew drunk and dizzy on it.
I walked down Market Street, down Castro,
went to movies and restaurants and bars.
I had a sense this might never end
and that was beautiful enough for me.

The silent film shows a city in love
with itself. Women with wide brimmed hats,
plumes of feathers arising like smoke
into the cool morning air. Autos and wagons
and streetcars passing in a barely ordered
chaos. In between, people walking randomly
across or down the street. In the distance,
the terminal's tower rises like a steeple
at the head of the bay.

Two Men Rowing Madly Toward Infinity

The current flows in the opposite direction
so they are moving, always,

       against.

Time is like water, but is not water.
Time flows, but isn't a river.
They're determined to reach their destination,
that point when they may turn the boat about
and head toward home. But oars drag slowly
through these viscous hours.
You cannot set your watch by it.
Better to use the sun, approximate
your position in the sky.
As they row, the shore becomes a series
of scrolling scenes, a diorama of one era
crashing into the next, an index
of possibilities. There is always the pull

        toward,

    which implies
its opposite. The push into one day
moves them

     away

        from another.

If there were such a thing,
one might say they've been in this boat

        forever.

But there's not, so they've always only just arrived.
It's a warm day on the river.
See how the light falls on their shoulders,
sweat glistening in the long sun.
Without the will to go forward,

they can only

    continue.

As the daylight ebbs, the dusk engulfs them.
In their vessel, the atoms of all that's

      been,

        all that

          is,

      all that

       will be

merge in the darkness, erase any difference between
the men, their craft, the water, and the endless world.

The Middle of Time

The North Road
      goes nowhere but north,
            guides the moon on her long journey,

eighteen and a half years
      from start to finish.
            Who can count this long?

I was born under the sign
      of the moon; last child,
            tenth of ten.

The next world is
      a perfect mirror of our own,
            so I am the middle child:

nine mortal children before me,
      nine spirit children after.
            I can hear their voices

from either side of the mirror
      so I have no home.
            Long before any of us

could walk, we could swim.
      Before we had feet,
            we had fins. Before lungs,

gills. We can never
      work the water out of us.
            The moon comes in her

perfect lines and pulls us
toward crazy, then toward calm.
The North Window allows no sun.

When the cycle is complete,
there's only moonlight
spilling across the stone floor.

Lie in bed, my love, admire
your reflection in the mirror,
but don't touch.

As each of my mother's
mortal children left,
her spirit children returned,

took their clothes, used
their beds. She became
so exhausted the house

fell down around her.
She had to escape the roof
that opened its arms to the sky.

The spirits stayed behind,
bound to the land.
When the house burned, they perished.

From a hundred miles away
I could hear them crying out.
There was nothing I could do.

The North Road runs to a canyon,
        then falls off. My life now
                is half on the road, half off,

scattered like broken pots
        at the bottom of the cliff.
                The next world is a perfect

mirror of our own.
        Look at your reflection
                long enough and you'll see

the face of each previous
        incarnation. You won't
                recognize anyone.

It's better not knowing.
        Reach into the mirror one night.
                You'll find a hand there

like your own,
        a perfect reflection,
                and it will hold you fast.

The Little Bird

Giotto's frescos of the life of Saint Francis
are still there, though shelling in the war
and the work of an earthquake have left them
in ruins. Yet, the work survives.
Francis grew up wealthy, gave away
everything he owned and removed himself
from the world. After, there was poverty,
contemplation, and an uncanny ability
to communicate with the animals.
The mantle of sanctity is a heavy burden,
enough to break a man's back.
Who can withstand it?
In one of the intact frescos,
a small brown bird is captured in flight.
It's a simple thing, a tiny wren,
pale brown against the plaster's inky blacks.
All of these centuries, it's been going
someplace, but, being mortal,
we'll never know where.
After Francis received the gifts from his god
and began to suffer as his savior suffered,
did the bird fly toward,
or away from, heaven?

A Thousand and Two Nights

She starts with the stars—celestial maps—
to guide the caravans and fleets.
But it's not enough, he's a greedy king,
so she moves on to the men, the beasts,
the women, the sands, the roads, the seas.
She learned a lifetime of stories from
her mother, and her mother before her.
It's no small feat to tell them.
Each thing on earth springs to life
as she speaks, but she speaks only
to appease the king so there's no
pleasure in it. When she's finished,
on the thousandth and one night,
the Sultan consents to spare her life.
She wants to sleep, but has forgotten
how to rest, so she decides there is
one more story to tell.

She starts with the stars—celestial maps—
and turns them off one by one.
The caravans are lost in desert sands
and the ships sail into the rocks
off the shores of uncharted territories.
She unmakes each animal, even man.
The sleeping Sultan doesn't notice
when the silk pillows dissolve
beneath his feet, when his slaves
turn to shadow, his castles
and temples into dust. Even her sisters
must make their retreat back

into the cosmic womb. She speaks herself,
last, out of existence; a relief after
a thousand and one nights for one king.
On the thousand and second night,
Scheherazade finally sets herself free.

Two Young Men in Another Country

From nooses tied to the arm of a crane, they hang.
This is the preferred method of execution, the newscaster says.

No steps to the gallows, no drop of the trap,
body falling, neck snapped.

Instead, a crane, with noose tied to a mechanical arm,
rope tightened around each man's neck,

steel arm raised so the men die slowly
as the crowd screams in approval.

If these men, eighteen, maybe twenty years old,
must die for who they are, may they have done

what they wanted to do. May their lips have known
one another, their tongues together, tangling slowly.

May they have seen one another naked, erect,
made love in the heat of the day, the light's rays

painted across their bodies. May theirs not be
a thwarted love, a longing only. Let them,

as the crane's arm raises, turn to face each other,
and leave this world with open, loving eyes.

On Martha Strawn's Porch

outside Davidson, NC

Jonathan Williams told me the birds
are sublime in North Carolina. The kind of birds

poets dream about when we do dream of birds.
And we do. Last night, I had a dream:

I was sitting with Martha on her long, narrow porch,
the one that looks down into the deep ravine,

then out into the dense, vine-clogged forest.
We were bird watching. I was looking

for the kinds of birds I cannot find up north
in Minnesota: tiny birds, bright as jewels,

their wings flashing orange and yellow and red
as they pass through the sharp, downward

shafts of sun. Mystical birds, the kind
that spring live from cautionary tales.

A blinding sweep of indigo and green
snapped into sight, moving toward us

at an impossible speed. Martha screamed
and I stood up, and the bird buried itself

in my chest, an empty cavity now filled
with feathers and blood and a winged heart.

I woke suddenly, sure something of the invisible world
was there in my room; perhaps a bird in the house,

or a snake under the bed, hiding the way they do,
like messengers from the darker realm,

the world we cannot run fast enough from
in our dreams.

The Night Horse

Distant, some miles, a field or two over,
a farm or two. Once, I knew every family
that lived up and down this country road,
who owned each farm, which of their kids
I'd gone to school with, what names
they had called me. I don't care now.
The horse, when it's neighing, may be
speaking to another, or speaking only
to itself, to the grassy pasture it inhabits.
The sound is drowned out, for a moment,
as the train passes by, two short whistle
blows to alert anyone near to step back.
The loose windowpanes, the door knobs,
every fixture in this house rattles
with the passing. There was a time
when I wouldn't have heard any of this,
my ears immune to sounds
I'd lived with for eighteen years,
crows and cows, fox cries, wind or rain.
Now, I hear it plainly, as I hear
the horse again, once the train passes.

The Summerland

You pass into sleep in the House of Pain,
in the room where wounds will no longer
heal, where the needle prick sends life
stringing back into your bloodstream.
It's a black and white dream,
a sad conflation of *The Wizard of Oz*
and *The Island of Lost Souls.*
Tornado's coming! shrieks the Leopard Girl,
while the Scarecrow and the Tin Man
scramble for the dinghy that will take them
back to the fog-drenched ship.
Get out! screams Dorothy, half-woman,
half-dog. *Get out while you still can!*

You wake to brilliant Technicolor.
Same bed, same room, but the tubes
and monitors are missing, no slow,
steady monitor's beat, only birdsong
and wind, deep green grass of the meadow
and the sky a transcendent shade of blue.
Same room but the walls are gone.
The house itself is gone. All of the sharp corners
are smoothed, the straight, slashing sounds,
the traffic, the sirens. Only bees fill the air.
You crawl from bed, fully healed, and head
to a village no one needs tell you about.
You spot your house and move in.
It's just that simple. The villagers don't talk
about heaven or hell. No one worries about sin.

Daily routines are enough to satisfy
and the pantries restock themselves
at night as you sleep. At first you worry
it's all a dream and will dissolve
back into the hospice room.
Then you worry that there's no need to worry.
Then, you forget. Forget what worry
was ever about. The weather's fine and
the summer's eternal. Such an autonomous
dream, this paradise. Listen to the wind
in the reeds along the lakeshore,
how they lash the air, how they sing.

Untitled Story (Poor)

The shuttered bar's wall collapses, falls into the Laundromat. Dirty clothes for days and nowhere to wash the oversized blankets, the heavy quilts stitched from remnants of Grandmother's dresses. Winter is coming so they get out the lath and heavy plastic. I knew families who lived like that, broken windows patched with canvas tarps, frozen breath forming clouds in the unheated kitchen. I knew families who depended on the meat their men would hunt each autumn. No game meant nothing to eat, shame-faced trips to the food shelves. A semblance of strength trumped the cries of a hungry child, and I would see those kids in the school hallways, pale and thin, lacking breakfast and focus. I was one of those kids, could always spot my kind, missing dead fathers, mothers eaten up by poor pay at local factories. Someone might ask: *how poor are you?* But you could not say, not to teachers, not to friends. Silence equaled strength, the ability to deny yourself everything. Those houses are empty now, bankrupt or abandoned, farmsteads unable to support any family. I see them on my way to visit my elderly mother. The animals take over, and trees grow up through kitchen floors. Upper bedrooms become aviaries, full of birds and owls that eat the birds, and bats sequestered in every corner.

Labor Day, Hague Avenue

The child across the street, practicing
his trombone, has trouble hitting

the right notes. The girl down the block
bounces her basketball on the sidewalk,

practices running jumps at invisible nets.
A neighbor cat has gone into heat,

adding her own off-key yowls
to the basketball's beat

and the tuneless trombone.
I walk the yard dead-heading flowers.

September is here. School's starting.
Already, a quiet has blanketed the neighborhood.

I'm less willing to speak when I have
more to say. Best to keep some notions

secret, locked away until they're useful.
I crumble dry flower heads to scatter

the seeds so next year's garden
will grow larger, more lush.

I listen to the trombone's slipping notes.
I'm content with the silence I keep.

S.O.S.

One rocket fails on the launch pad.
Another succeeds.
　　　　　　Then, a dog in space.
A monkey in space.
　　　　　　Nameless men
and women in space.
　　　　　　A lost radio
S.O.S. from a Soviet rocket, a woman
screaming that the ship is on fire,
is picked up on a ham radio by
a lonely man in the middle of the U.S.

Then, silence.
　　　　　　Darkness is her grave.
We must let them go.
　　　　　　History may
keep them, but we forget history.

A friend said, no one is dead
as long as the living remember.

I don't know how long that is.

The universe is eternal, but starlight
is dead.
　　　　You and I alone in
our capsule. We finally run out of
things to say.
　　　　　　And so we sleep,
surrounded, as we are, by silence.

The Night Horse: New Poems

Vigil, Bedside

Rain's darkness yet, no rain.
    Only the back and forthness
        of sun and cloud, sun under cloud, sun, no cloud.

The heat makes this contrariness unbearable.
    Ferns doze in the worst of it, what ferns still stand,
        and the air is tension, anticipation.

Housebound, but self-imposed, hiding from
    what I will not accept, cannot accommodate,
        this dew-soaked air, the exhaustion of breathing.

All through the house, the scent of hot attic musk,
    dust-choked, mildewed, rotting.
        We're waiting for something but we must not say what.

She sleeps through most of the day
    and when she wakes, she stays near the window,
        looking out, patient, knowing.

I make deals with the devils that inhabit my head,
    as if I have the power to will anything into action.
        These devils never sleep, always eat, are eternally hungry.

Say it out loud! But I must not.
    Words possess the power to make things happen,
        like wishing for an end to suffering, then it ends.

I am wishing for an end that is inevitable but will not come.
    But I want it to. There, it's said. And so the days stretch
        impossibly thin, brittle, until she, at last, with the heat, breaks.

As breath in winter

As breath in winter, issuing from our mouths, vaporous, that delicate.
As a string holding the witch ball in the window, that thin.
As the earliest flowers, those that grow up through the snow, that tenacious.
As the fog over the marsh, thick, white, that diaphanous.

The catkins bloomed early in the false spring, then died in the frost.
We opened windows we should not have, just to hear the new birds.
A white cat jumps from the fence to the garage roof each morning,
      paces its slope.

By nighttime the neighborhood has closed its blinds.
An open window is an invitation to peer in, take away a little of someone
      else's life.
I hang blackout curtains in the bedroom, not to block the light,
but to stop greedy eyes from looking in.
The wind rattles the loose panes all winter long.

As a shudder in a cup of water when a cat strides by, that subtle.
As the world looks bent and spotted through my glasses, that warped.
As long as I can remember, I'll remember it, that long.
As a hand hovering over my own, though not touching, that heat.

Perfect

Nothing is perfect, except, perhaps, the ice,
the way it quietly cracks as the waiter
refills my water glass, and the sun, filtering
down through the newly emerging locust leaves,
refracts in the cold fissures, and turns
a simple glass into a vessel full of light.

None of us has a right to expect perfection.
It's rarely there, and to expect it is to sacrifice
the honest joy we feel when such it is achieved.
My eyes, for instance, are not flawless,
nor his chin, nor my hair. Our shirts are, generally,
wrinkled, our clothes, frumpy, and the food
we eat is only routine, despite the pristine reputation
of the restaurant upon whose patio we now sit,
despite the outrageous cost of everything
on the menu, despite our unspoken hope
that the food will be sublime.

This isn't April in Paris. It's May in Saint Paul.
The beautiful tulips that border the walls
around the patio seem to strive for transcendence,
but cannot achieve it. The scent of the newly
thawed earth does not give off a perfumed bouquet,
but it's pungently familiar, and comforting.
What's perfect is the fact that the sun
has travelled back to us again,
and it dazzles me as it fills my glass.

Mourning Doves

I suppose their call is melancholy, though
I've never found it so. Or, more precisely,
I've never found it out of place on quiet
summer days, because there is a sense
of melancholy stitched into the season.
The whole world goes wild in bloom;
trees leaf-out to the point of bursting;
the air's scent is cut grass and clover
heating in the high sun. This can't last.
It's a celebration in the manner that
the dance of death is a celebration—
a nod to the inevitability of transformation.
A mourning dove calls out. It sounds
utterly alone, though it isn't. It sings,
perhaps, of a love that lasts beyond loss.
I share with my mother a tenderness
for lesser beauty, whatever is ragtag,
slightly frayed, leftover, or abandoned.
We love the birds without splendid
plumage, the animals left after the storm,
all of those who sing into the distance,
and hope that someone answers back.

The Angels' Alphabet

The clouds, split along thin,
jagged lines, form

a text of some kind, maybe
the angels' alphabet,

a divine language
I'll never comprehend.

On bright days, the sunlight
plays over the fresh-plowed

fields, and the soil seems
to move in waves, some lighter,

some darker, and if there
are clouds, their shadows

cast themselves across
the land, the rolling hills

that look so much like
a dark ocean. I know

there are many who
have drowned in this

endless flatness, fallen
into that green sea

and never resurfaced.
How easy, if you don't

know the pattern of
the fertile tides,

to be taken in by them,
held down, pulled under.

American Fairy Tale

Here is something we dreamed up,
a tired nation's collective id:
old and orange and angry.

Here's a leader that no one wants,
a one percent man, a greedy thing
that never ceases to devour.

Here is a cabinet full of horrors,
no surprise there, just plenty of
stupidity, rigidity, repetition.

Here's a man not worth a cent, not worth
a pence, an old white pot to piss in,
narrow little man in a narrow little door.

Here is a church. Here is a steeple.
Open the doors and herd all of
the people into debtor's prisons.

Here's a nightmare we all had, a thing
we thought we'd escaped in our sleep.
Now it's a waking killer, a wicked king.

Morning/Mourning (2013)

The two words, wed. Each, a beginning,
what starts a new day, what comes at the end

of a darkness. Moving toward death takes you
deeper into night. Death, then, is dawn.

I see her but don't. She's here because
I believe she's here. Faith's a weak thing,

demands too long a wait for proof.
I've learned well. My teachers are proud.

I take nothing on faith. If A, then B.
But life doesn't follow logic's lead.

It was too hot that July when I turned
fifty. I found her the morning after.

She had climbed to the window.
Maybe she saw a guide there,

and went to greet him. Her new body
passed through the glass.

The old one remained, a hollow husk.

Oculus

I. Oculus

To see, she opens her body

Across the mountain, valley
to peak, she wanders between
one world and another

Milky gaze

Visionary

The eye, in shape, resembles
the mouth

To see:
            one object, then
the next

No continuous flow, but
a series of notes stitched

Can she sing, in her seeing,
the shape of the whole world?

II. UnRest

No blessing to be many-eyed

Ask Cerberus

No sleep, no hour when
        all of those eyes close

Seeing everything, there is no
        mystery in the world

No secret I do not know

Sometimes, knowledge
        is a blade that cuts
        thin and deep

Deep enough to bifurcate
        the soul

III. Venus of Willenburg

Underneath every thing, another thing

History's strings pull at skin and
make the body not taut, but softer

There is a great deal I could say
about everyday life: childbirth,
seed sowing, a house full of fruit and grain

But I won't

No one would listen and I can't care

Let me talk instead about the stars

I've seen them in my dreams; I've visited them

Lived there among the born and the unborn

Every eye that has seen me has left its mark
on my skin

Never mind

In the future, I will be beautiful

The Librarian

(Marcel Duchamp at the Bibliotèque Sainte-Geneviève)

wishbone   swan neck   violin   naked back
    willow branch   broken glass   fierce ant   bridal veil

catalogued, call numbered, shelved according to an intricate system
of letters and numbers and symbols only the librarian can understand
no substitutes allowed
the stacks are closed when he is away

dog's breath   baby hair   funeral wreath   white fox
     fair game   gamelan   broken tile   promise ring

a archives hold a file for everyone who has lived   he has
named them all
every unborn child and all of those born
everybody, nobody, somebody, orphan
organize infinity, then let it go
what survives spins out of control

he picks up the call cards one by one, groups them according to an
atavistic dream

everything connects: bow tie   baby buggy   lion's head
    one hundred days   fur covered tea cup and spoon plate glass
        giant wheel   swan lights

Paris night as it comes on, at dusk the sky a specific shade of blue

a doll hangs in the window of a house beside a highway in the middle
    of winter

stars lost amidst the clouds

the sky filled with a million swallows, their wings darkening the air
    above Rome

wrought iron ring   holy relic   snakeskin   thumb tack
        shoelace   broken glass   hairline   flimflam

The Night Loves the Night

The night loves the night, and so it compounds,
building upon itself, carrying the dark structures

and the dark streets on its back like a dowager's
hump. Nightfall by four in the afternoon,

snow pellets strike the windows, a constant
snare drum, endless staccato. Tomorrow,

everything will be painted in ice.

The night loves the night, and so it grows
in the frozen soil, roots too shallow to hold

yet taller every hour, a vine with fine fingers
stretching over the side of a house. If you don't

see this, that which moves toward you
with incredible speed will overtake you,

and bring on a blankness remarkable, and deep.

The night loves the night, like marries like,
and in that love, grows beyond all reckoning.

A salted road, a dirty car, wind rattling
a chain link fence, and all along the freeway,

stars blooming from streetlamps, drawing
their bright arcs across the winter sky,

falling the way stars do, silently, splendidly.

Through Birds, Through Fire, But Not Through Glass

after Yves Tanguy

I have come all this way to see you.

Over great concrete highways, down dirt roads, gravel roads and no roads at all. Paths and trails where the animals walk, through forests, prairie, desert, mountain.

Through the air, as a bird, as I used to dream I was a bird. Through fog and rain, snow and heat, the ground below me shimmering. Over clouds and through the haze of a million smoke stacks, rancid air burning my throat, lungs, eyes.

Across time zones, war zones, continents, across nations, invisible nations, eradicated nations, across settled land, contested land and the little land untouched, unseen.

Down silt-filled wide rivers, wild rocky rivers, down streams, across lakes, so many lakes, great lakes and small, mud lakes, loon lakes and even the lake of heaven.

Through wires and cable, through circuits smaller than a single cell, through machines, cogs, wheels, foundries, factories, through the very waves of the air, choked with secrets.

Over oceans, islands, sand, snow. Through fire that flares up from fissures, volcanoes, through lava, magma and the infinitely burning earth's core.

I have come to tell you what I've seen, but now I can't describe it.

I was born with only one tongue and its language is poor. When I speak: feathers, not words. Something like Babel but something worse. You cannot translate an object, not even one as light as a feather, into language. Not into your language, beautiful as the sun, whispers and roaring all at once, more complex than any other thing in this world.

I've come to you in this body, weak thing, tangle of muscle, tendon, bone, sorry blood and a heart scarred, useless. This empty body, ready for the grave. I've pushed it across miles, through time, fires, houses buried. I've ridden it until blood ran from my eyes, until my feet, dry as clay, disintegrated under me.

I've come to say what I need to say to you, a poor man with pockets full of air, whose mind is locked by pills so strong no dream can escape: no thought, no question, silent in the face of all that's clear. A man whose body will not pass through glass, who does not have a ticket, who may not board the train he needs in order to save his life.

The sun is setting behind an alabaster scrim. We see only shadows where there should be mirrors, open windows. I know you from the shape you are, the height, as you move through the milky light. I move toward you as you move away. A clumsy dance.

A Bird, A Plane

Each goes in its own direction,
crossing paths only long enough
to sketch an invisible X
in the early morning sky.
The bird is singular,
not part of a flock flying
toward another spring.
A hawk, or an eagle, its eyes
sharp, razor talons poised
to strike any little life
on the ground. When I
was a child, I thought
planes only flew away
from me, as those from
the nearby army base
passed overhead, breaking
the sound barrier so the air
itself shook; they wrote themselves,
in white plumes, out of sight.
The planes I see now mean
something else. The possibility
of escape, or, a potential for terror.
The plane disappears and
I thank the sky for keeping it.
The bird circles once more,
then vanishes into the bright day.

Tinnitus (in Four Movements)

I.

The summer I turned
seventeen, the cicadas
woke from their long sleep
and crawled up through
the ground, flew up to
the trees, and began to sing.
Their song was constant,
like the raging green outside
and the damp summer heat.

II.

As a child I thought
I was a machine.
The endless ringing
in my ears, proof of
the intricate wires
and gears that threaded
through me, always turning.

III.

I thought I had caught
this singing from
the cicadas, a contagion
of sound, my constant,
mad companion.

IV.

John Cage, I read, entered
a laboratory chamber where,

scientists said, there was silence.
But his body was made of sound.
There was no escape from
the pulse of his own blood.
He called it *deafening*.

First Photograph of a Snowflake

Wilson Alwyn Bentley, Circa 1910
Metropolitan Museum of Art, New York

Their chief property: impermanence.
What one discovers must be
quickly preserved.

The chief challenges: scale and speed.
How to capture a single flake, magnify
it hundreds of times, be certain that

the intact image is burned onto
the large glass negative, all accomplished
in the dark of the blackout hood.

The primary goal: to create an image
clean and clear, free of motion when,
by nature, the flake is only motion.

He tries it hundreds of times,
the microscope, the camera,
the hot keg lights blasting hard.

Finally, the contradictions hold
and the ephemeral is captured.
When he makes a positive and drops

the paper into the developer,
he watches as winter itself emerges,
intricate and perfect.

Impossible Ballad

I. One Bright Day

All of it sheer, thin as anything can be without breaking;
this is how the air seems, a fragile bubble, ready to pop.
The heat, unwavering, constant, like the sun, but meaner.
We go blind as we walk through the trees. Even the trees
and their canopies cannot save us, and the leaves
are in flame, suddenly erupting, then gone, almost like
a ghost. In Iceland, they build roads around those places
where the little ones live, the fairies, the sprites.
They have many names, and they're elemental things,
good and bad. The roads are built around their rock houses
because to anger one is to risk the worst wrath, a curse
that rises from deep inside our own bones, from the genes
we share with the rocks, the grass, the sea. When it grows
angry, we wither, we die. But the trees we walk under,
those that always gave shade, today offer nothing but flames.
What comes next is inevitable, but still, we must choose.
Look into those caves over there in the hills.
Some are at ground level, some perched up high,
small holes in the sheer granite face. See how dark it is
in those recesses, those cool doorways. We'll walk into them
because we must, but we still must choose, and in choosing
we join our ancestors, those who lived in fear of the dark,
who invented the fire that drives us back to that dusky cold.

II. In the Middle of the Night

There are no stars because there's too much light.
Sometimes, there's Venus. Always, the moon.
And there are planes, and satellites, all the invisible things
spinning wildly over our heads, filling every cubic inch
of air with information, images, our own endless chatter.
Someone is always listening, always recording.
We've learned this recently. No phone call goes unnoticed,
noted down in a Doomsday Book about which we
know nothing, only that it's being written every day
as our lives themselves are being written. What will
anyone do with all that information?
The streetlights are spotlights that mark out
the sidewalk's path. Run from puddle to puddle of light,
bow in the illuminated circle of each. Maybe someone
will see you, record it, then report it. Maybe no one
will notice, and then it will be as if it never happened.

III. Two Dead Boys

If I am a contradiction of nature, then so is he.
I can't remember my first birth, but I know what
the second was like, a cold, sudden snap of the neck,
but backward, from darkness into light, breathlessness
into breath, and burning, everywhere I looked, it was burning.
Just the sun. But what if you had been hidden away
from the sun for longer than you can remember, a day
or a year or even an eternity, there's just no knowing

because that's the point, the bliss of nothingness.
And then awake! Pulled up from the ground like a plant
plucked up by the roots. No root loves the light, though
the light may feed it. No root is meant to live above ground.
Yet, there I was. Shocking to the world and more than
shocked by it. He was there too. I knew him when we were
…boys? I can't find the words. If you don't use language,
you lose it, and much of mine still lies in peace. Once,
I was here in this hot, blinding world. And he
was here too. Much like me, confused. I had to squint
so hard to see it because my eyes wanted to refuse.
But there was something in his eyes, in mine.
Was it anger, or hatred? We looked at one another.
We knew, without being told, what we had to do,
though we didn't know, would never know, why.

IV. Got Up to Fight

I wouldn't want this world if you gave it to me.
So take it back. I'd hand it to you if I could.
Take it back. I refuse your offer. Power's never
meant much to me, though powerlessness is
something I've wrestled with all my life.
Maybe this is lack of ambition or direction.
Maybe this is a lack of faith. But no one will find
these elements if they seek them. They are like
small objects lost in the house, a common word
that slips your mind and you know you know it
and you know you'll never remember it as long

as you keep trying. So forget it. Tomorrow, when
you're doing something else, the word will come.

It will arrive abruptly, in the middle of thinking about
anything else. And that lost object, a ring or a key or
a button, it will be found under your shoe or in a drawer.
Nothing that exists will cease to exist. Things change form.
There are the living and there are the dead and usually,
it's not a wide step between one and the other. We see
each other or we don't, but we inhabit the same space.
Think of it: every moment as you pass from room to
room, you walk through the middle of someone else's life,
their reality, their mortality. They do the same to you.
It's not enough that we must endure this crowdedness,
a planet literally spilling over with lives in their multiple
phases. We cannot change it. There are laws and
there are laws and this one is fixed. No ticket to talk
your way out of, no free pass, no bond. We're in this
together, forever, so make some space. I'm coming through.

American Dream:
The Brief Life and Glorious Death of Klaus Nomi

One: Pastry Chef (1978)

An artist in New York must cobble together
an adequate living, just enough to cover
the rent for a cheap SoHo efficiency,
with something set aside for costumes,
makeup, and food. Drinks are always
on the house, or find their way onto
a strangers tab; staggering, what a drunk man
will pay for at the end of the evening.
I find my way into someone's bed
less often than I'd like, but I've discovered
that a minimum of contact with maximum
visibility makes one more mysterious.
Weekdays, I bake pastries at
The World Trade Center. I know
the intricate decorations on a cake
must be crafted carefully as a costume,
with a little artistic wiggle room, but no mistakes.
My eclairs are heavenly, and hold
an impossible abundance of sweet buttercream.
My birthday cakes are Byzantine,
spun sugar lace and an array of marzipan
flowers so marvelous they rival the gardens
at Givenchy. It takes an alien operatic queen
to conjure such exquisite desserts.
Sometimes, I take the intricate patterns
I create for my cakes and turn them
into costumes, but only I know
that the flowing plastic gown I wore

at the club last week was borrowed
directly from a cake I'd baked;
the only thing missing, on stage,
was the "Happy Birthday, Buffy!"
and those words should have been traced,
in royal icing, across my trim little ass.

Two: SNL 1979

Everyone will be watching because
this is David Bowie's first time on the show.
Everyone wants to know what he'll wear,
what he'll sing, whether or not he's still
high as kite. The public savors cataclysms,
and many who watch will be hoping for
a cocaine-fueled meltdown. Well.
Mr. Bowie will disappoint the doubters.
I'm told he's been clean since Berlin.
This is my own television debut.
I crave the chance to be seen by millions.
Bowed lips and top knot, white face, black suit
cinched tight at the waist. I'm a trim man,
not skinny (not yet) not fat, just fit.
Bowie will wear a long blue woolen skirt
with a matching jacket and shoes for the first song,
and the fantastic fiberglass Bauhaus suit
for the second. Joey Arias and I will have to carry
David out for that number, set him on his mark
at the mic. All he will be able to move are his arms;

otherwise, he'll resemble a turtle on its back,
limbs clawing helplessly in the air.
I covet that Oscar Schlemer suit but
cannot afford it on a backup singer's salary.
There are never great lyrics for the chorus.
These are reserved for the star. I know my part
by heart, some extended *oohs!, ahs!* and *Who knows?*
Not me! for "The Man Who Sold the World,"
and later *boys, boys, boys keep swinging,*
boys always work it out! The guitar solo
in that song grinds on my nerves.
The hot keg lights threaten to melt my white
pancake makeup. Some have said it makes me
look like a sad little clown, but that comes with
the territory when you're an alien on earth,
an interloper among men. When the applause
comes, it's wild and loud and I close my eyes
and pretend it's for an aria I've just performed,
and all of that adoration is just for me.

Three: Total Eclipse

A slip of color, just enough to suggest
the arched line of my brow.
Who is the *It Girl* now, Clara Bow?
Me!
Who is the one everyone at the disco
wants to know?
Me!

It's marvelous being an object of desire.
I'd felt it so rarely that when it began,
I didn't know how to react;
unexpected adulation is intimidating.
Yet the record company wanted me, so I signed.
Who am I so say no to Lady Fortuna?
When they said I needed a hit single,
I sang what they gave me. Some silly song
about the end of the world. *Total Eclipse.*
I started the song as a tenor, but when
the chorus came, I was a diva, all soprano.
Fall out, nobody left to crawl out
If someone calls we're all out
Turning into French fries…
Total eclipse! It's a total eclipse!
It's a total eclipse of the sun!
The sound shocked, but had a beat.
With my carefully constructed alien demeanor,
I was the new Queen of the Night.
The discos went wild with it. Powered up
by fine white powder and pink champagne,
I took every stage I stepped on by storm.
New York, Paris, London, Berlin.
Moving from stage haunt to headliner
had always been my dream.
In the blinding spotlights of every stage,
I could never see the audience,
but they all screamed my name.

Four: Performing "The Cold Song"
Munich, Germany, 1982

> *What Power art thou who from below*
> *Hast made me rise unwillingly and slow*
> *From beds of everlasting snow?*
> *John Dryden*

I'll die in New York. I will not die here.
This is just a stopover to say goodbye
to my mother. This is just a chance to sing
my swan song, to prove my worth to this
undeserving nation. I selected "The Cold Song"
from Purcell's *King Arthur* because cold is what
I felt growing up here amidst angry former
Nazis and shell-shocked civilians.
I was born in the ruins of war, my mother
crouching in the basement of a bombed
out hospital, as the doctors, their hands
still bloody from the battlefields, pulled me
into the world. It was ugly, but I was not.

> *See'st thou not how stiff and wondrous old,*
> *Far unfit to bear the bitter cold,*
> *I can scarcely move or draw my breath?*

The concert hall is filled to capacity.
Are they all here to see me flourish
or fail? My Renaissance doublet
is immaculate and the tights and ruff

hide Kaposi's fleur du mal blooming
across my body. Thick, white makeup
hides a face paler still, gaunt, splendid.
My receding hairline is Elizabethan.
My lungs don't possess the capacity
they once did, and prolonged singing
exhausts me, but I was born to play
this role, the epitome of vanquished
beauty, a masculinity shaped by finely
tailored layers of brocade and attitude.
I walk on stage to delicious applause.
This is what gives me life in my long dying.

Let me, let me freeze again to death.

Five: The Assumption
New York, Summer 1983

It's the beauty in the world that makes life worth living.
Never mind the taunts as I walk down the street.
I look like a skeleton because I am a skeleton
on the inside, all of us are, and time makes us
equally transparent in the end.
My skin has grown as diaphanous as the gowns
I wore when I sang the aria from *Daphnis et Chloe*
at CBGB's. How they all stared. They'd never heard
a countertenor. I loved it. Why remain a talented tenor
when you can sing the soprano's song and become the diva

you've always known you are? I left one country
in search of another, and found New York instead.
There can be no other city. Concrete, steel, and stone
are the skin of the gorgeous underneath, the luxurious
darkness, the pleasure of pain, the eternal singing.
Can you hear it? Each of us must, in turn, open
our mouths wide in song, swallow what's given.
There's little to explain now that I'm alone.
Those who loved me loved a shimmering facade,
an alien in the form of a man. They loved the clownish
pancake makeup, the beautiful totality of nothingness.
But I can only be myself in this bed,
now that my legs are weak, my lungs unable
to breathe without making that most unmusical
sound, a halting rattle. I was only a simple German boy
who wanted to be a queen from outer space,
like Zsa Zsa Gabor in that science fiction film.
I was enchantment itself when I sang, but
all those pure notes have fallen on god's deaf ears,
so now I am silent. I'm friendless. I wait.
Soon there will be splendidly-robed angels,
and all around me, a gorgeous, heavenly chorus,
backing me up, singing me home.

Miranda Castle
Celles, Belgium

Because fairy tales never die, they must leave
each building before it collapses, travel in
the night sky over the endless forest, and find
a new home. The old home becomes uninhabitable.
Who could endure such a multi-storied life,
the myriad ghosts that must fill such a structure.
The witch is gone, but her spirit lives on.
The dwarfs in spectral form march up and down
the corridors all night long. Even the princess lingers,
a spirit caught in a nether-place between royalty
and wretch. She's still waiting, always
will wait, for that prince, the one who grew
old without her, and died in another woman's arms.
The beautiful arched ceilings collapse.
Delicate plasterwork falls to the floor, and
the floor itself, warped by eons of summer heat
and winter cold, rolls like a hilly landscape up
and down, impossible to traverse. The long
dark hallways, designed to fit the flow of silk
and velvet gowns that had to drift through them,
are a carpet of dust and debris; ghosts leave
no footprints, so there's nothing to document
their airy comings and goings, just the rustle
of dry leaves, flaking paint, phantom brocade.
The grand stairwell has seen the worst of it.
Chipped marble, unfinished by rain and time,
can offer only unsettled ascent, not the elegant
descent of the queen as she glides down
the polished steps, her dainty feet invisible
under a satin gown, so she seems to float

to her guests, a deity among mortals.
The broken first floor windows, the vines
that sheath the rock walls and grow into the castle,
small trees sprouting on the parapets, tell us
no one is in residence now, in the palace where
desire and imagination wed and bore
their ragtag band of children.

Not Finding

Each shadow holds your shape

You inhabit a nuanced darkness

I am looking for you everywhere

Nowhere is the place I find you

Your face in the outline of the leaves

Your eyes in the gas station lights
      that shine like daytime all night long

Your voice in every voice I hear

You've come to live inside my ear
      a small, constant, ringing

Behind my eyes, your own

The Monster Addresses His Maker
on the Night of His Nuptials

You have fled so far from me that you've run
out of land. You've tried to cross over the top
of the world with your bride. You have failed.
The moment you gave life to me, you became
my beloved. I'm the product of your rib,
Adam born from Adam. You might know
her body, might possess it momentarily,
but you created me, birthed me from the refuse
of the dead. My arms were always meant to
embrace you. In her cabin, she lies cold
as snow, too fragile to survive this rough world.
But my hide is thicker, my body equal only
to yours. See the glacier field, how it stretches
on for miles, disappears into the mouth of the sky?
I've made a wedding chamber there for the two of us.
When they drove me from the village I learned
to live among the trees. Now I crave stillness.
When your legs grow too tired to walk, I'll carry you.
There in the ice, we'll find our perfect balance,
and make our marriage bed our grave.

American Fairy Tale II: President Fabulous

I don't think this new president is mine.
Maybe the last one was, but now he's out
on the links, puttering away what's left of
his life. I don't know if there has ever
been a president for me and my kind.
Who is the president of all us little sissies?
Who is president of all of us tomboys,
tough women, weak-wristed men? For all of us
strung so beautifully along the sexual continuum,
every one of us, gendered, non-gendered,
quasi-gendered, multi-gendered, omni-all-
and-everything-in-between-gendered?
Who is the president of the queers?
Who is the leader of our free queer world?
I know this new president is not.
I know he's not the president of anything
other than the art of the (bad) deal, art of the steal,
art of the oligarchy of privileged white men
with no imagination and too much cash.
He's not my president if he can't shake his hips,
won't put his lips on any part of another man,
won't raise his legs above his head in that
last, sweet salute. I want a president of the United States
of the Diaphanous, the United States of the Dangerous,
the United States of the Dull, the Fascinating, the Genius,
and the Dumbfounded. A president of the boys, the bois,
the grrrrls, the women, the womyn, the ladies,
the great, the small, a president for all of us who know,
under the current regime, we have no voice.

The Night Horse

The darkness is a river.
The horse runs through it,

determined, blind.
For him, there's no rest.

The dusk is a kite
tied to his tail.

As he moves deeper
into the forest,

he tries to outrun
his edgeless burden.

Stars illuminate
flanks black with sweat,

and thick muscles ripple
like water under shadow-skin.

He loves the dawn best,
when the darkness cracks,

but he'll never catch
his twin, that bright star.

Fierce eyes pierce what's left
of daylight and he breathes

the last of it in. He shines hard
and bright in the moonlight,

this last horse.
He exhales the night.

On the Microscopic Structure of Tears

I

Water loves water. Spring to stream,
stream to river, river to ocean.
It all begins and ends in the same sea.
Our bodies are mostly water and
we bleed salty water. Grief washes
down through our tear ducts,
thin creek, pool of consequence.
When have we ever severed the hold
the ancient oceans have on us?
Walk into the sea and still, the waves
will love you without end,
the tide will cradle you till you sleep.

II

Dense at the core, like the walls of an ancient,
buried city where the stones refuse change,
despite the ruthless onslaught of wind and sand.
There has to be something of the original
that remains, a vessel to contain memory,
store it for the time when our human minds
refuse to retain anything so distant as
one thousand years, ten thousand years.
Every house around the core is shattered.
Those walls remember only that they were sand,
are sand, were changed only long enough
to fall into smaller and smaller pieces.

III

With the intrusion of the square, the death
of the curvilinear. A grand stamp
on the land as a claim to ownership.
This wall here, that wall there,
and a grand palace for the victor.
Even children know how the game
of square peg, round hole begins
and ends, a frustration that insists
someone must win, someone, lose.

IV

Aerial view of a small town:
Two roads intersecting, First and Main,
the only paved streets. Stands of oak
and maple remain from what was once
a vast hardwood forest. This is the kind
of place you'd end up only if you got lost.
East of nowhere, a long haul down
a gravel road with nothing at the end
but a few broken streets, old stores
long shuttered, gas station gone,
grocery store gone, everything gone
but your parents' graves, and grief,
hard and bitter enough to hold you.

V

At last, the ice goes out. Those who
live along the shore tell us
the sound is like a great groaning.
Sometimes it all happens so fast
that the vast sheets of ice strike
the shore and burrow under
the grass. This provides some relief.
Spring returns, and even those
who love the cold will laugh at
the sky on the first warm day.

The Poison Garden at Alnwick Castle

Guarding the gates to a garden behind
a castle in Northumberland, is a skull
and crossbones on an ornate fence,
with a sign that reads: *These Plants Can Kill.*
The Medici's grew such a garden behind
their palazzo, discreetly tucked between
the medicinal plants and the herbarium.
Kill not heal could have been their motto.
No one cares that aspirin comes
from tree bark, but tell them that
Angel's Trumpet is an aphrodisiac
with deadly consequences and
they'll line up to look at the long white
blossoms that Victorian ladies kept
in their nightstands because just a pinch
in their evening tea was enough to
send them on a hot, wild trip.
In medieval Scotland, soporific sponges
soaked in henbane were used
to heal wounds, and hemlock
to anesthetize patients before amputations.
Sometimes, poison is the best medicine.
If you crave sleep in the middle
of the night, ingest Datura and you'll
sleep forever, or lie in a pile
of fresh-pruned laurel leaves
and you'll silently drift into death.
A British woman in the 1890's
was told that the scent of too many lilies
could kill. Feeling suicidal but

craving beauty, she arranged
for her bedroom to be filled
with hundreds of lilies, then retired
for the night. When she woke
the next morning, she knew all
about quackery. The most common
are usually the killers, innocuous
weeds, pale things growing
under a canopy of trees,
those green things we mindlessly
step on, pull up, and throw away.

American Fairy Tale III:
Tonight Will Be the Darkest Night in Nearly 500 Years

A lunar eclipse on the longest night of the year
will turn this night into a slow wake for winter.
What we hope for each autumn is a reprieve,
a mild December or January. This year, what we
hope for is survival. The country has gone dark
under the shadow of hate, and a politician suggests
the laws be changed to reflect the moral lack
of the president elect. I don't want to understand
what post-truth means, but I suspect I know.
What can any of us do with this darkness
on a night like this? How can we ever light
enough lamps to make up for what the sun
cannot give us? Ethical people are turning away
at the thought of this new menace slouching
toward the capital. Good people are gathering up
every scrap of compassion they can find so
the world won't run dry during the coming season.
Struggle as we will, there's a path set and
we have to follow it, even in our sad dissent.
As the moon disappears behind the great shadow,
I'll mourn its loss, but remember that after
these long, black hours, the equinox comes.

Notes and Acknowledgments

The poems in this volume were originally published in the following books:

An Alchemy in the Bones
New Rivers Press
Minneapolis, MN
1999
(newriverspress.com)

How To: Poems
Mid-List Press
Minneapolis, MN
2004

This Brightness: Poems
Mid-List Press
Minneapolis, MN 2007
2007

Sin Eater: Poems
Mid-List Press
Minneapolis, MN
2010

As breath in winter
MIEL Press
Ghent, Belgium
2015
(miel.bigcartel.com)

*Two Men Rowing Madly
Toward Infinity*
Broadstone Books
Frankfort, KY
2016
(broadstonebooks.com)

"A Torn Curtain" is for Brett Klinker
"Now That We Are Never Finished Mourning" is in memory of Mark
    Miller
"Hypothesis: Love" is for Judy Swatosh
"Black Mountain, Ten Perspectives" is for Thomas Meyer, and in mem-
    ory of Jonathan Williams
"Clara's Vision" is in memory of Clara "Kitty" Couch

"Wrapped: Red" is for Pinky Bass

"As breath in winter," "Oculus," "The Librarian," and "Through Birds, Through Fire, But Not Through Glass" originally appeared in *As breath in winter*, a limited edition chapbook published by MIEL Press, Ghent, Belgium, 2015.

A special thank you to the members of my writing group: James Cihlar, Greg Hewett, and Christopher Tradowsky.

Many thanks to Larry Moore at Broadstone Books.

Much gratitude to Marianne Nora and Lane Stiles, founders/publishers of Mid-List Press. They were my publishing home for many years. The pressed closed in 2017.

My gratitude and love to Jonis Agee and Brent Spencer, founders of Brighthorse Books and longtime friends.

The following poems, from *The Night Horse: New Poems*, previously appeared in these publications:

"A Bird, A Plane" in *Metafore*

"The Poison Garden at Alnwick Castle" in *Panoplyzine*

"First Photograph of a Snowflake" and "American Fairy Tale" in *Sheila-Na-Gig*

"American Dream: The Brief Life and Glorious Death of Klaus Nomi" in *Assaracus*

"Mourning/Mourning (2013)" in *Soul-Lit*

"Vigil, Bedside" in *Pinyon Poetry*

ABOUT THE AUTHOR

WILLIAM REICHARD is a Minnesota-born writer, editor, and educator. He holds a BA in Film Studies, an MA in Creative Writing, and a PhD in 20th Century American Literature. He is the author of five poetry collections, two chapbooks, and an anthology of poetry, fiction, and creative nonfiction by contemporary American authors that focuses on social justice and social change issues. A frequent collaborator with artists from other fields, he's won several local and national awards and fellowships for his writing. He is an English instructor at Inver Hills Community College and lives in Saint Paul, MN, with his spouse, poet James Cihlar.